Frederick County Characters

Innovators, Pioneers & Patriots
of Western Maryland

JOHN W. ASHBURY

FOREWORD BY CHRISTOPHER HAUGH

THE
History
PRESS

Published by The History Press
Charleston, SC 29403
www.historypress.net

Copyright © 2013 by John W. Ashbury
All rights reserved

First published 2013

Manufactured in the United States

ISBN 978.1.62619.266.9

Library of Congress CIP data applied for.

To all the men and women past and present who have made Frederick, both city and county—and the nation—a place of remarkable achievement in the history of our great country.

…and to my wife, Gaile, whose patience and understanding of my passion for local history has made it so much easier to pursue.

Contents

CONTENTS

Contents

Foreword

Saying John Ashbury is passionate about Frederick County's history is a vast understatement. If the study of a place and its people can be a religious experience, he is a devout fanatic seated in the church's first pew. What's more, John is not afraid to take to the pulpit from time to time, whether called upon or not. A fitting analogy, considering our subject is the son of an Episcopal minister.

I first met John in C. Burr Artz Library in 1994. Fittingly, we were behind microfilm readers, eyes blurry from hours sifting through early Frederick newspapers. At that time, I was researching for a film documentary called *Frederick Town*, a Ken Burns approach to our county seat's history that would eventually run on local cable television. Meanwhile, John was compiling hundreds of date-driven happenings (and supporting facts) for a daily series of "History Moments" that he eventually provided to WFMD throughout 1995. (In a few short years, these would be expanded to compose a hard- and soft-cover book.) We were in essence doing like tasks, seeking information to help teach Frederick history to audiences over our mass mediums in conjunction with the City of Frederick's 250th anniversary commemoration. More importantly, we had the same burning interest in Frederick's past and a desire to learn more for ourselves. Pretty ironic since we are both "Frederick outsiders," being native-born Virginians.

The roots for John's local history craving date back to the early 1950s as he listened for hours on end to stories told to his parents by lifelong Fredericktonians. Among the "local bards" in the parsonage of All Saints

Episcopal Church were Judge Edward S. Delaplaine, Arthur Potts and Parsons Newman, to name a few. Armed with a love for words and storytelling, it's no surprise that John would earn a college degree as an English major with a minor in history and Greek. He would embark on a career in journalism and editorial, pursuits that included newspapers ranging from the *Frederick News-Post, Raleigh News & Observer, Baltimore Sun, Bloomington Tribune, Roanoke World-News, Frederick Gazette* and *Glade Times and Mountain Mirror.*

Nearly twenty years after our first meeting, John and I continue to find ourselves in the storytelling vocation—me with Frederick County Tourism and John through continued research and writing for books, magazine articles and the Internet. We also find ourselves as kindred spirits, connected to the same "inspirationalists." As I mentioned earlier, John's love of local history was originally sparked by local historian Edward Delaplaine, where I produced *Frederick Town* and three additional historical documentaries under the guidance and employ of Judge Delaplaine's nephew, George B. Delaplaine Jr. John's "History Moments" radio project was encouraged by WFMD's former program director, John Fieseler. Today, Mr. Fieseler is in his fifteenth year as executive director of the Tourism Council of Frederick County, Inc., and has been my boss for the last seven. And along the way, John Ashbury occasionally hosted a successful local political crosstalk program entitled *Pressing Issues* on the former cable TV channel that the Delaplaine family owned and I managed.

Throughout the years, we have routinely singled each other out for advice and counsel on subject matter and approaches to be taken. No matter the format, we still love learning, researching and telling Frederick's story to others and each other. I have always admired John's tenacity, outspokenness and ability to debate topics when necessary. I myself exhibit these traits, and in the pursuit of public history, they certainly aid us in illustrating a person or event's impact on future generations. I, however, continue to learn from John, who has refined these skills with fifty-plus years of experience.

In my opinion, John's greatest public history achievement to date was to organize and chronicle those items plucked from microfilm and countless books and pamphlets at the time I met him back in 1994. Four years of microfilm research led to a daybook-style masterpiece entitled *...and all our yesterdays: A Chronicle of Frederick County, Maryland.* The book's back cover describes the work as "a treasure trove of little known facts and amusing anecdotes of life in mid-Maryland's largest county." To the thousands who own a copy or have referenced this book at a library, it is truly something to be treasured. I personally own three copies and refer to it weekly.

With that said, I am truly honored to play a small role in this, John Ashbury's latest history project, another "must-have" resource for those interested in Frederick history. This compilation includes forty-seven articles previously written for *Frederick Magazine* since 2005. Also included are three pieces he contributed to another Frederick history, *Pillars of Frederick* (2011). Many of these pieces have, as their subjects, names that once graced the local community but have faded in both importance and prominence—historical underdogs who fought their way to state and national greatness, along with "communal angels" who simply fell from grace. With additional knowledge and experience in politics and business, John has been well equipped in exploring and explaining the political and socioeconomic legacy of past characters ranging from Frederick's first citizen, Joseph D. Baker, to canning magnate Louis McMurray to inventor extraordinaire McClintock Young.

And it's not always the people who represent greatness and have had a positive impact on our community. John has studied the dark flipside, our least upstanding of citizens and innocent victims of tragic events. These have included notorious local criminal cases such as the murders of the Newey family of Harbaugh Valley, terrible accidents and all those individuals who have been publicly executed and/or lynched.

Many historians revel in exploring the famed "what if" question and how the course of a community changes based on an event happening or a different decision being made by a person in power. John thrives on this. He is not only a gifted storyteller but also a connection maker and strategist. He can effectively illustrate the impact of events, decisions and the outcomes they bring. Or, for those decisions not made, what the outcome could or would have been. We are talking about history research in reverse, using the knowledge of the current day as a lens to view through, filled with countless connections to other persons and events. This is a trademark of John's articles.

One of the most interesting things about John is that he sees the events and people that surround us today as the subject and research of future historians looking back at our time period. As good as he is at unraveling history, he is just as good at predicting it. This current work will be a tremendous research aid for current and future researchers. Years of John Ashbury's articles on the good, the bad and the ugly can be found here for the taking. Put simply, this book is another "treasure trove" and heavenly reward for all of us.

Christopher Haugh
Documentary Filmmaker and Scenic Byways and Special Projects Manager
Tourism Council of Frederick County

Acknowledgements

No one can ever thank all those who have contributed to whatever success they may have attained. Or even those who ignited a lifelong interest in something that has remained since those early days growing up.

Both of my parents were gifted educators who insisted that their children "pay attention." We did, not from fear of a spanking or something more severe but because of the love they had for us and also the love they had for their chosen professions, teacher and minister—Frances Walker Ashbury and the Reverend Maurice Dunbar Ashbury.

When my father became rector of All Saints Episcopal Church in Frederick, it was the custom of the parishioners to call on the new rector. It was through these visits that a lifelong passion for Frederick County's illustrious history was ignited. Judge Edward S. Delaplaine, noted jurist and local historian of books on the life and times of Thomas Johnson, Maryland's first governor, and Francis Scott Key; Arthur Potts, who lived across Courthouse Square from the rectory; Harry Decker, in whose memory the Historical Society of Frederick County established an essay contest for local fourth grade students; and Parsons Newman, who served the local historical society in numerous capacities, all came to call. For some reason, I didn't leave the room while these "old people" talked. I sprawled on the living room floor, fascinated by their tales of Frederick's history.

After college, I spent years looking for a "new and better" place to live. I never found it, so my wife and family came back "home," immediately renewing my fascination with local history.

In 1994, as the 250th anniversary of the founding of Frederick City approached, both John Fieseler, morning radio host at WFMD 930AM, and his boss, Michael Gibbons, asked me to write one-minute pieces on the city's history to be broadcast five days a week during the city's celebration. When that work was completed, it was suggested by several people that I write a book on both the city's and county's history to be published in 1997 for the 250th anniversary of the establishment of Frederick County …*and all our yesterdays: A Chronicle of Frederick County, Maryland* was the result. Tom Gorsline, publisher of *Frederick Magazine* and owner of Diversions Publications, produced that volume, reigniting his own passion for our local history. It was a few years later that he asked me to write articles for his magazine. This current volume is a collection of forty-seven of those articles, plus three additional items written for *Pillars of Frederick* in 2011.

Through the years, I have collected hundreds of books, pamphlets, newspaper articles and photographs dealing with local events. But no collection can ever provide all the information you need. You find things everywhere, from archives at the Historical Society of Frederick County and the Maryland Room of the C. Burr Artz Library to casual conversations with longtime residents—and even some newcomers who have heard things and want to know more.

Mary Mannix, manager of the Maryland Room, and her associate Carolyn Magura continue to this day to be of great assistance. Both epitomize what gracious public servants can be. There is never a complaint about what they are asked to do, and they always return phone calls to point you in the right direction to find what you need.

Chris Haugh, Scenic Byways and Special Projects manager for the Tourism Council of Frederick County, has always been someone I can turn to for lively conversation about our history. His passion is greater than my own, and his research is far superior to mine as well. My old friend from WFMD 930AM, John Fieseler, is now the director of the Tourism Council, demonstrating his own continued interest in local history.

Rebecca Crago, director of the Research Center, and Duane Doxzen, assistant director of the Historical Society of Frederick County, and those who have gone before them at the society have helped me immensely.

Others who deserve special acknowledgement include: Thomas John Chew Williams and Folger McKinsey, authors of *History of Frederick County*; Matthew Page Andrews, who wrote and/or compiled the four volumes of *Tercentenary History of Maryland*; the Knott family, now of Baltimore County, whose origins are in Urbana; DePauw University of Greencastle, Indiana;

Mount Saint Mary's University of Emmitsburg, Maryland; the writings of Judge Delaplaine published in the *Frederick News-Post*; George B. Delaplaine Jr., longtime publisher of the *News-Post*; Marlene Young, who headed up the committee that published *Pillars of Frederick* in 2011; Yemi, a local artist, who frequently sought information on local history and provided the artwork for three of the pioneers contained in this volume; G. Thomas Mills Sr. and his wife, Marg, who provided the inspiration to continue writing after some years' absence; old and dear friends Paul and Rita Gordon, who published a volume on local history for the county's schoolchildren, providing a jumping-off point for every researcher of events here; Tom Summers, longtime head of the Francis Scott Key Memorial Association; and his daughter, Julie Summers Walker, without whose editing skill, assistance and guidance this volume would be only a pipe dream.

There are hundreds of people who have expressed interest in our county's history and forced me to do additional research to answer their questions. Especial thanks to the Frederick Coffee Club membership, whose interest in local events and history sparked many a discussion—and additional research—into the county's glorious history.

Thank you to graphic artists Matthew Piersall and Joseph Weyman, who took time from their duties at Diversions Publications to locate and reproduce much of the artwork in this volume—a hearty nod of the head for a job well done.

And to Joseph Silovich and Shawn Dewees, owners of Diversion Publications and publishers of *Frederick Magazine*, thanks for allowing me to create the short biographies contained herein and for permission to have them reproduced.

A special thank-you to Karen Trout Reed, my niece, who never denies me her services in bolstering my enthusiasm for local history and provides me with expert advice on graphics and publishing. I really don't know what I would do without her.

And finally, here's a special and deep-felt thank-you to all the men and women of Frederick County, whether born and raised here or who moved here and made Frederick County a place we can truly call "home." And to those who were born here and moved away to ply their trade or to pursue another path, we will be forever grateful, for you have demonstrated that the seeds planted in your heart as a child grew to magnificent heights elsewhere.

Introduction

I suppose there are other places with a rich history not unlike what we find right here in Frederick County. You can walk the streets of even the smallest of communities and feel the pull of those who have gone before and left their mark. But unlike other places, the people—and I mean all of them—in Frederick County celebrate that history and uncover more and more of the unique events and personages that have made this place such a treasure-trove of exciting happenings and special people.

From earliest days, these have included men such as Thomas Johnson, a true Patriot of the American Revolution and first governor of the Free State, and women like Margaret Byrd Rawson, the Grande Dame of Dyslexia, who chose to retire in Frederick after a life of giving to those afflicted with this malady.

Then there is McClintock Young, whose inventions kept Ox Fibre Brush Company among the nation's manufacturing leaders fifty years after his death in 1913. Holmes Davenport Baker and Emory L. Coblentz were born and raised here and led the local banking industry for generations. The legacy of Miss Emily Johnson, the daughter of a renowned physician and an unassuming lady, engendered hundreds of children through a nursery school she ran long before such facilities became the norm.

There were educators like Joseph Henry Apple Jr., who led Hood College for forty-one years, and John Casper Henry Dielman, professor at Mount Saint Mary's College, who became the first in America to be awarded a doctorate of music. And William O. Lee Jr., a physical education teacher at the all-Negro Lincoln High School, who rose to be a principal and later a Frederick City alderman.

And journalists abound. L. Victor Baughman published the *Citizen* for many years before entering politics as Maryland comptroller. Thomas John Chew Williams and Folger McKinsey wrote and edited what is known as Williams's *History of Frederick County*.

The attorneys so excelled that their names grace the pages of not only Maryland history but national as well—from Thomas Stone, who signed the Declaration of Independence, to Luther Martin, who was Maryland's attorney general for more than thirty years and defended Aaron Burr in his trial for treason. And lest we forget, there was Leo Weinberg, so gifted an orator that when he argued a case before the Maryland Court of Appeals, other local lawyers closed their offices and traveled to Annapolis just to hear his presentation. Glenn H. Worthington, who as a child witnessed the Battle of Monocacy, became a local jurist and later penned the definitive narrative of "The Battle that Saved Washington" during the Civil War. James McSherry became chief judge of the Maryland Court of Appeals, and Enoch Louis Lowe rose so quickly in state politics that he became Maryland governor at age thirty.

Local merchants' names ring in our ears even today. Men like Casper Ezra Cline, who bought his first furnishings business at just sixteen years old and became a household name through much of the twentieth century. Charles Baltzell Rouss, who was born in Woodsboro, became the Colossus of New York. Louis McMurray invented a process to hermetically seal packaging and operated perhaps the largest packing plant in Frederick's long history. Then there was James H. Gambrill Jr., who inherited a mill from his father and grew the business to untold heights, providing hardtack for World War I soldiers.

Local philanthropists abound, perhaps none more prominent than Samuel H. Rosenstock, whose gifts to Hood College, Frederick Memorial Hospital and the Salvation Army won't soon be forgotten. John Loats willed his property to a local church for the establishment of an orphanage that descended into scholarships for local students attending Maryland colleges and universities.

The military heroes of today almost pale in the glow of those Frederick County men who went before—Revolutionary War men like Roger Nelson, Lawrence Everhart, Otho Holland Williams and James Wilkinson; David Geisinger in the War of 1812; Bradley T. Johnson and William Nelson Pendleton in the Civil War; Admiral Winfield Scott Schley in the Spanish-

American War; and Randolph Russell Waesche, who was born in Thurmont and became head of the United States Coast Guard during World War II.

And we can't leave out the physicians who served our communities, men like John Tyler, who performed the first cataract surgery in this part of the country and perhaps in all the nation. Victor F. Cullen's recovery from tuberculosis led to his lifelong devotion to those with this dreaded disease; William Schnauffer III was a gifted surgeon who founded a hospital in Brunswick, his hometown; and Bernard O. Thomas Sr. delivered both the first and last babies to be born in the old Montevue Hospital.

There are others included in this volume—some whose names you will know and others, plucked from the obscurity of history, who left an indelible mark on our beloved county. They will all resonate when you read their stories.

Authors

THOMAS JOHN CHEW WILLIAMS
Newspaperman and Distinguished Historian

Who is this man whose name you hear so often when discussing Frederick County history? How did he happen to write *History of Frederick County*? And why was Folger McKinsey, the Bentztown Bard, selected as co-author?

Looking back now more than 150 years after his birth, even the barest of details about Thomas John Chew Williams are difficult to find. He was born on a five-hundred-acre tobacco farm in Calvert County, the son of the Reverend Henry Williams, a native of Hagerstown, and Priscilla Chew Williams, the granddaughter of Bishop Thomas John Clagett, the first church prelate consecrated on American soil. Less than a year after Thomas was born, his father died, leaving a widow and five children, the oldest of whom was just twelve.

Over the next several years, the family moved frequently, first to a home in Prince George's County, then to the Clagett homeplace and then back to the farm. Life was a struggle, and the boys received only a minimal formal education. Tom Williams's first school was three miles from home and would play a significant role many years later when he taught there for three years.

Just sixteen years old when he began teaching, he wanted something more, so he studied law and was admitted to the bar in Prince George's when he was just twenty. However, there was little in the way of legal work there,

Thomas John Chew Williams. *From Williams,* History of Frederick County.

so he moved to Hagerstown, where many in his mother's family resided. Another likely reason for the move was Cora Maddox, another descendant of Bishop Clagett, and his cousin.

It wasn't long before he had the opportunity to buy into the *Mail,* Hagerstown's weekly newspaper. It was a fortuitous move, for it led him eventually to Baltimore's *Sun,* where he worked with the aforementioned McKinsey. Williams's years as an editorial writer for the *Mail* brought him a solid reputation for common sense, honesty and integrity. He became friends with some of the most powerful men in Maryland.

After a few years, and his marriage to Miss Maddox and the birth of his children, Williams moved to Baltimore on Election Day 1891, fifteen years before McKinsey arrived there. He was first assigned to Annapolis to cover the General Assembly. His endeavors met with such favor that he was appointed to the two commissions that oversaw the construction of a new building for the legislators and the renovation and updating of the state's capitol.

Through all these years, Williams was greatly interested in history, particularly that of Washington County, Maryland. In 1906, the year McKinsey joined the *Sun*, Williams published *History of Washington County*. And although he had never lived in Frederick County, he was prodded by many to write a history of that county. He and McKinsey made an agreement that McKinsey would write Frederick County's history from 1860 to the time of publication, and Williams would cover the years prior. Williams had the easier side of the project because Washington County was part of Frederick County until 1777. After the successful venture came to fruition in 1910, Williams collaborated with James W. Thomas in gathering material and writing *History of Allegheny County*.

In the same year that *History of Frederick County* was published, Williams was appointed the first judge in Maryland to be assigned to strictly juvenile cases. Both Democratic and Republican governors kept him in that position until he resigned in May 1929 because of the continued failure of his eyesight.

Williams enjoyed semi-retirement, keeping active with the affairs of his church: Baltimore's St. Michaels and All Angels. After attending a vestry meeting, he complained that he did not feel well and suddenly collapsed. He died shortly afterward, on December 11, 1929.

Knowing something about the man somehow makes one's appreciation of his work all the more fascinating. Every student in Frederick County should read Williams's work. It not only provides an insight into Frederick County's history but also provides a portrait of a man devoted to preserving the past for the future.

Bankers

HOLMES DAVENPORT BAKER

Banker, Conservationist and Philanthropist

He was ahead of his time in espousing conservation issues and proved himself a worthy successor to his father as president of Citizens National Bank. His involvement in the community reflected his passion for his hometown, its progress and its improvement.

Holmes Davenport Baker was born in Frederick on April 11, 1880, the son of "Frederick's First Citizen"—Joseph Dill Baker—and Emma Cunningham Baker, a native of Falling Waters, West Virginia. He lost his mother when he was just two years old. His father then married Virginia Markell, the daughter of a prominent Baltimore family, in 1890.

After graduating from local schools, Baker attended Western Maryland College in Westminster, from which he graduated in 1899. Active in sports, he captained the football team in 1898. After completing business courses in Baltimore, he joined Citizens as a clerk on January 11, 1899, rising through the ranks to succeed his father as president in 1922, a position he held at the time of his death on April 15, 1950, in Baltimore.

Shortly after replacing his father as president, he married Geraldine Frost of New York City on September 16, 1922. So active in the community, it would seem that his time at home would be limited. However, his son, Joseph

Holmes Davenport Baker. *From* Tercentenary History of Maryland.

D. Baker II, recalls that he was gentle, friendly, always positive in his outlook and never very political. That recollection was shared by his contemporaries. A City of Frederick resolution upon his death said that "he was a citizen who was always available and one could rely upon his opinion being free of political expedience or personal gain. In numerous and untold instances, his words of caution were a vital force in the problems that confronted this community."

Baker shared the passion of his good friend James H. Gambrill Jr. for conservation. He was a member of the State Board of Geology, Mines and Water Resources and a past president and active member of Friends of the Land for Maryland. As the *Frederick Post* said in his obituary, "With him, conservation of all natural resources was a virtual hobby."

His involvement in the Frederick community reflected his era. He was a member of the Chamber of Commerce, a charter member of the Rotary Club of Frederick, a vice-president of the Union Manufacturing Company, a member of the Board of Directors of the Potomac Edison Company, a vice-president of the Buckingham School at Buckeystown, a member of the Board of Trustees of Hood College and the Home for the Aged and a member of the Federal Reserve Board of Baltimore. He actively supported the local Community Chest and the Red Cross.

Baker served in the U.S. Army's Quartermaster Corps during World War I, attaining the rank of captain. During World War II, he was chairman of the Frederick County Rationing Board.

He was also philanthropic. He and his sister, Charlotte Markell Baker King, donated the William R. Diggs Pool at Mullinix Park in honor of a longtime family employee. There were other gifts made for the betterment of the community, but many were made quietly, reflecting his unassuming personality.

One of his proudest accomplishments was his part in the building of the Francis Scott Key Hotel in downtown Frederick. He was a charter member of the Frederick Hotel Company as he worked diligently to promote and sell the stock that funded its construction. He served as vice-president from its establishment until 1949, when he was elected president.

Few in the community knew of Baker's hospitalization at Baltimore's Union Memorial, and all were shocked by his untimely death. His wife survived, as did his son and a daughter, now Mrs. Geraldine Cooper of Crestwood, Kentucky. His sister, Mrs. King, and several nieces and nephews also survived. Following services at All Saints Episcopal Church, where he had served many years as vestryman, he was laid to rest at Mount Olivet Cemetery.

Emory Lorenzo Coblentz

Educator, Attorney and Champion of His Community

Perhaps no individual in the history of Frederick County was more vilified than Emory Lorenzo Coblentz, a denigration that overshadowed his many good works.

Born November 5, 1869, into a farm family in the Middletown Valley, he rose to prominence in just about every business venture in the county from 1887 until his death in 1941. But for the failure of the bank he headed, he may have gone down in local history as a folk hero whose Midas touch was sought after by business leaders across the region and Maryland.

He was educated in the one-room Deer Spring School and was among the first students and graduates of Middletown High School. His early ambition was to be a teacher, but his business acumen drew him to other pursuits. Instead of attending Franklin & Marshall College, he accepted a position as assistant cashier of the Valley Savings Bank in 1887, an introduction to a business that eventually caused him great personal loss and pain.

In the mid-1890s, he read for the law with Charles W. Ross in Frederick and was among the first to take a written bar exam as required by an 1896 state law. Eventually, he garnered a successful practice, dealing primarily in equity

and testamentary law. He was the first Frederick attorney to employ a stenographer. Many fledgling firms sought his counsel. He advised on both legal and business matters such companies as Ox Fibre Brush Company, Economy Silo and Manufacturing, the Frederick & Hagerstown Railway, several insurance companies and not just a few financial institutions. He was also the most prominent organizer of the Potomac Edison Company.

In 1919, he was elected to the Maryland House of Delegates, where he became the father of the state's lateral roads system. He served one term in the House but was elected a state senator in 1930. Upon his retirement from state government, he was appointed to the State Board of Education, a post he held until his death.

Top: Emory Lorenzo Coblentz. *From Williams*, History of Frederick County.

Bottom: Emory Lorenzo Coblentz. *From* Tercentenary History of Maryland.

But it was as a banker that most will remember Emory Coblentz—and not fondly. Coblentz rose rapidly in banking circles, in particular with the Central National Bank, which became the Central Trust Company, moving from Court and Church Streets to North Market and Church Streets, into a sparkling new four-story structure.

Anyone who has read about the 1920s knows it was a time of great real estate investments and growth in the banking industry. It was this combination that led, in part, to the crash of the stock market in 1929 and the beginnings of the Great Depression. As real estate foreclosures mounted, Coblentz attempted to save his bank with more than $1.5 million of his own funds. It didn't help much, and on September 3, 1931, Central Trust shuttered its doors and those of its fourteen branches, trapping $14 million in depositors' funds, including that of Coblentz.

From then until his death on August 6, 1941, Coblentz was a pariah in all of Frederick County. People even spat on him as they passed on the street. But some who knew him said he maintained a cherry outlook and continued to work other avenues for the benefit of citizens throughout the county. At his church, Middletown's Christ Reformed, Coblentz continued his heavy involvement. He was an accomplished musician and even compiled a hymnal for the Sunday school.

Today, the primary visible evidence of his presence in our community is Coblentz Hall at Hood College. He had served as a trustee for many years and was instrumental in raising the funds necessary to build the structure. Just to list the accomplishments of Coblentz as a lawyer, banker, musician, legislator, churchman, organizer and public-spirited citizen would take several pages. Suffice it to say that few, if any, did as much for the betterment of our community as he.

Criminals

THE MURDER OF CONSTABLE JOHN R. LLOYD
Still Unsolved

In the days of the Old West, with outlaws running rampant, it wasn't unusual to see reward posters everywhere you looked, particularly outside the sheriff's office. In Frederick County, monetary compensation leading to the arrest and conviction of a murderer was a rare event, especially in a case that remains unresolved to this day—sixty-eight years later.

It has long been claimed that the only law enforcement official ever killed in the line of duty was Deputy Sheriff Clyde L. Hauver, who was gunned down during a raid on a whiskey still west of Thurmont. His killers were arrested, convicted and served long prison terms.

However, the case of the murder of County Constable John R. Lloyd is unique in the county's history. Constable Lloyd had many years of service in law enforcement following his service in Europe during World War I. He had been a deputy sheriff for some years prior to a railroad accident that resulted in the amputation of both legs. He then became a constable, charged with serving legal papers for the county courts.

On the evening of April 27, 1945, just before midnight, Mr. Lloyd had just taken a seat in his living room, preparing to listen to a radio program. A blast from a shotgun through a window struck him in the neck and the right side of his head. His sister, Mrs. Ella Ruble, with whom he lived, rushed into the

SHERIFF'S OFFICE OF FREDERICK COUNTY

FREDERICK, MARYLAND

August 10, 1945

$1,000 REWARD

WANTED FOR MURDER

Reward of $1,000.00 is offered by the County Commissioners of Frederick County for information leading to the arrest and conviction of the person or persons who killed John R. Lloyd a County Constable of Frederick County, at his home near Brunswick, Maryland. Mr. Lloyd on the night of April 27, 1945, was sitting in the living room of his home when a charge of No. 6 shot was fired through a porch window on the first floor of the dwelling house. This charge of shot struck Mr. Lloyd in the right side of his face and head, from which he died instantly. The extension butt plate to the stock of the shotgun probably used by the murderer was found near the scene and can be seen upon application to the Sheriff of Frederick County.

Whoever furnishes information leading to the arrest and conviction of the guilty person or persons will be fully protected. Information will be received in absolute confidence.

Members of all Police Agencies are asked to make every effort to obtain any information that might lead to the solution of this crime. Information may be communicated in person or by telephone or telegraph, collect, to the Sheriff's Office of Frederick County. Information may be given to the Sheriff, and constable of Frederick County or to any member of the Maryland State Police Department.

HORACE M. ALEXANDER,
Sheriff of Frederick County, Maryland

State's Attorney's Office
of Frederick County
Tel. Frederick 63

Sheriff's Office
of Frederick County
Tel. Frederick 261

Maryland State Police Barracks
Frederick, Maryland
Telephone 101

Reward poster in death of John Lloyd. *From the author's collection.*

room from a rear porch where she was putting away some empty canning jars and found him slumped in the chair. Mrs. Ruble awakened a boarder, George Babington, a brakeman for the Baltimore and Ohio Railroad. He called the Brunswick Police and the State Police in Frederick. Dr. William

Schnauffer, who at the time operated a hospital in Brunswick, hurried to the scene on the old Brunswick–Point of Rocks Road but was unable to revive Mr. Lloyd.

Law enforcement officials from across the county rushed to the scene, hoping to develop clues that would lead to a speedy arrest. The only one located was a butt plate from a shotgun found near a fence the perpetrator lost as he made his escape.

As the months dragged on, the investigation ground to a halt. Officials from as far away as Texas, including the Federal Bureau of Investigation, were involved, but no substantial suspect was identified. Sheriff Horace "Buck" Alexander, exasperated by the lack of progress in the case, appealed to the county commissioners to offer a reward. On July 23, 1945, they did so, adding to a contribution from local attorney Sherman P. Bowers, posting a $1,000 reward for the arrest and conviction of the murderer. The commissioners told Sheriff Alexander to print and distribute handbills and circulars stating the details of the reward. It was never claimed, and the case remains open to this day.

Following funeral services at Lloyd's home and at the First Reformed Church in Brunswick, Lloyd was buried in the Reformed Cemetery in Jefferson. He was survived by a brother, Ernest C. Lloyd, and two sisters, Mrs. Ruble and Mrs. Eva H. Bobo of Washington.

In a shocking coincidence, ten years later almost to the day, Magistrate Charles Leslie Moats was shot and killed in the basement of his Brunswick home. The killer, also using a shotgun, fired at Magistrate Moats through a window on April 23, 1955. As far as could be determined, this case also remains unsolved, again despite a reward being offered.

THE NEWEY-MARKLEY MURDERS

A Most Unusual Case

When George Flautt woke his sons on the morning of December 31, 1830, he harbored a horrifying secret, one that would not be revealed for more than thirty years.

That morning, Flautt's wife looked out her kitchen window in their Harbaugh Valley farmhouse toward the home of their closest neighbor, John Newey. She called to her husband, saying that there appeared to be smoke rising from Newey's house. John Flautt, their eldest son, was dispatched to investigate. Shortly, he was back spreading the alarm that the house was engulfed in flames. When the flames died down, Newey's entire family—his wife, children and father-in-law—and an apprentice were dead, murdered by an unknown assailant.

Suspicion quickly fell at the feet of Newey's nephew, John Markley, who had sworn revenge for testimony by Newey that had sent him to jail five years earlier. When arrested in Baltimore in late January 1831, Markley was in possession of numerous items identified as belonging to Newey or other members of the Newey household.

Markley's trial began on Wednesday, May 18, 1831, with State's Attorney James Dixon presenting a wholly circumstantial case before Judge John Buchanan. William Ross and Joseph Palmer defended Markley. The primary evidence against Markley was a pair of pantaloons known to have been Newey's because of a patch in them done with white thread and, of course, Markley's threats five years earlier.

On the second day of the trial, the jury returned a verdict of guilty of the murder of John Newey, the only victim named in the indictment. Two days later, Judge Buchanan sentenced Markey to be hanged for the crime.

On June 24, 1831, John Markley was executed on the grounds of the Hessian Barracks, an event witnessed by more than four thousand people. Even as the noose was fitted around his neck and despite the pleas of the Reverend David Frederick Schaeffer, pastor of the Evangelical Lutheran Church, that he go to "his Maker" with a clear conscience, Markley refused to claim responsibility for the murders and arson.

After he was pronounced dead, his body was lowered to a concealed area beneath the gallows where local physicians performed an immediate autopsy, hoping to uncover some medical reason for the heinous crime.

Five years later, George Flautt sold his Harbaugh Valley farm and moved to southern Ohio to be closer to some of his older children. For unknown reasons, all of George's relatives changed their names to Floyd. Perhaps it was done to escape any connection to the Newey murders, which had been news across the burgeoning country.

More than thirty years passed before anyone paid much attention to George Flautt (Floyd). Then an article appeared in the *Cincinnati Commercial Appeal* in January 1867. A fairly inaccurate account of the Newey murders was followed by a statement from a physician who said he had attended a man on his deathbed who gave a detailed description of the murders, the fire, the trial and the execution of John Markley.

The doctor said he was told that Flautt and John Newey had been friends up until Flautt lost a lawsuit in which Newey testified against his position. Flautt revealed that his anger led him to murder Newey and his family and to cast the blame in the direction of John Markley. The doctor said his dying patient offered minute details of how he committed the murders and set the house on fire. He said that he had invited Markley to sleep in his barn, and when he went to awaken him the next morning, he slipped Newey's belongings into the unsuspecting Markley's bag. He then sent him on his way before he went into his house and followed his usual routine.

The doctor never revealed his patient's name, but the details of the crime were so specific, and fit what was known to a tee, that only the actual murderer could have made such a deathbed confession. Besides, this man said he lived closest to the Neweys at the time of the murders; thus, it had to be George Flautt, who had changed his name to Floyd.

Educators

JOSEPH HENRY APPLE JR.
Progenitor of Hood College

Perhaps no one with connections to Frederick has had a greater influence on higher education than Joseph Henry Apple Jr., president of Hood College from its founding in 1893 as the Women's College of Frederick to his retirement in July 1934. However, his association with the college is only a small part of the story of this fabled educator.

During his forty-one-year tenure as president, the college grew from a small boarding school with eighty-three students in the old Frederick Female Seminary on East Church Street to one occupying a twenty-eight-acre site on Frederick's western edge with more than five hundred students. The construction of numerous buildings—all of which are still in use—was done during his presidency. Until 1930, the Winchester Hall facilities in downtown Frederick were used as dormitories.

Before and after his association with the college, Dr. Apple was an avid musician, playing in brass bands and singing with choral groups, one of which performed at the Chicago World's Fair in 1893. He lent his voice to numerous church choirs through the years. After becoming an ordained minister in 1933, he was a popular guest preacher in Reformed churches in Maryland, Pennsylvania and Ohio until after World War II.

Perhaps it was the influence of his parents and their siblings that led Dr. Apple to such varied interests. His father was a Reformed minister, and his mother was the daughter of a minister who served a church in Manchester, Maryland, for thirty-one years. His father's brothers carried on varied careers, as might be expected. One was an amateur astronomer and photographer who later became director of the Daniel Scholl Observatory at Franklin & Marshall College. Another was a successful insurance agent, yet another was a watchmaker and jeweler. His mother's father, the Reverend Jacob Geiger, in addition to being a pastor, was the first homeopathic physician to practice in Maryland. Ten of his descendants also became homeopathic doctors.

Top: Joseph Henry Apple in 1893. *From Williams,* History of Frederick County.

Bottom: Joseph Henry Apple Jr. in retirement. *Courtesy of Hood College.*

Dr. Apple was also interested in athletics. As a teacher at Central High School in Clarion, Pennsylvania, he "stimulated" the gymnastics program and was involved in coaching various other sports. Before and after he graduated Phi Beta Kappa from Franklin & Marshall, he was a member of the Pennsylvania National Guard, rising from private to sergeant during his ten-year enlistment from 1880 to 1890.

When he was president of Hood, he took an active interest in libraries, perhaps because for most of his years at the college, there was only the Frederick County Free Library, which had no permanent location until the C. Burr Artz Library opened in 1937. Dr. Apple became a member of the Maryland Public Library Commission in 1912 and became its president in 1917. He was still the head of that body when he retired.

His military training and service led him naturally to the chairmanship of the campaign committee for the erection of a memorial to those Frederick County men and women who served in World War I. The stature of *Liberty* in Memorial Grounds Park at Second and Bentz Streets in Frederick is a constant reminder of the work of the committee, headed by Hammond Urner.

Married twice, Dr. Apple was the father of four children, two by each wife. His first wife died in 1896 after a lingering illness. Two years later, he remarried. All four children, and two grandchildren, survived his death on January 17, 1948. He was buried at Mount Olivet Cemetery after services in Broadbeck Hall on the Hood campus.

On October 12, 1940, the cornerstone was laid for the Joseph Henry Apple Jr. Library. It was dedicated the next year. Currently, this building is called the Apple Academic Resource Center and is across the street from the Beneficial-Hodson Library.

JOHN CASPER HENRY DIELMAN
A Life of Note and Talented Composition

In the mid-nineteenth century, it was not unusual for students at Mount Saint Mary's College to remain in their dorms during holiday seasons, bringing an unexpected treat to freshmen. Dr. John Casper Henry Dielman, the first American composer to be awarded a doctorate of music, would awake the sleeping students by marching through the halls playing "Adeste Fidelis" on his violin—or perhaps on any number of instruments of which he was a master. It was a tradition that ended with Henry Dielman's death in 1882. There was another tradition of his that continued until 1921, when his son Larry was too ill to walk to his father's grave playing that same tune on the flute.

Henry Dielman was born on April 26, 1810, at Frankfort-on-the-Main, Germany, the son of John Casper Dielman, a noted musician at the time. Early on, he displayed a musical talent beyond that of his father, so much so that his training was placed first in the hands of Monsieur Femmey, a first-rate violinist, and later with Hofreth Anthony Andre, court musician to the Duke of Isenburg. Dr. Dielman became so accomplished that at age seventeen, he was invited to become first violinist with a Philadelphia opera company, a position he filled for two years. He then went to Baltimore, where he was surrounded by influential friends, attracted not only by his musical talents but also by his character and his teaching skills.

John Casper Henry Dielman. *Courtesy of Mount Saint Mary's University.*

While he led several choirs, he continued to compose, following up on "Inaugural Marches," composed shortly after arriving in America. These were played at the swearing-in of several presidents, from Andrew Jackson through Andrew Johnson. When William Henry Harrison died just a month into his term, Dr. Dielman composed a funeral march. He previously had composed a solemn march upon the death of the Marquis de Lafayette.

In 1843, he accepted a professorship at Mount Saint Mary's College. He was but thirty-three. The years that followed benefited the entire region, as his music and his teaching abilities inspired countless numbers to attend his concerts and his church, where he played the organ for nearly forty years.

In 1849, Georgetown University conferred a doctor of music degree on Henry Dielman, the first such award to an individual in America. General Zachary Taylor, who was president at the time, presented the degree at elaborate ceremonies in Washington, D.C. Another unexpected honor came from Pope Pius IX, who bestowed a silver medal on Dr. Dielman "for meritorious composition." It was delivered by Vincennes (Indiana) bishop Francis Chatard, a former student at the Mount, who had received the medal directly from the pope.

After several weeks of illness in the late summer of 1882, Dr. Dielman passed into history. But his son, Larry, a master of the banjo, walked to his father's grave near the Grotto of Lourdes playing the flute, one of his father's favorite instruments. He often said that he mastered the flute to honor his father. Although he owned a general merchandise store in Emmitsburg, Larry Dielman never forsook his musical training, for he frequently entertained his customers with little "ditties" he composed—often including people from the community.

The funeral of Dr. Dielman was lavish in its simplicity. The organ in his church remained silent, draped in mourning as if to express its own sorrow at the passing of the man who played such wonderful praise on its keys for nearly forty years.

From one obituary came this fitting tribute: "The head of the great genius is laid low resting on a pillow of dust, the lute is silent, the harp strings are broken, but around the sacred mound which hides him from our sight, will cluster tender memories and holy associations, the reward of a life crowned with beauty and grandeur, and the approval of all who knew him."

MISS EMILY JOHNSON
The Legacy of a "Lady"

There are houses all over Frederick with stories buried within their walls. Spite House on West Church Street is a prime example. However, in the 100 block of North Bentz Street are three homes built to allow their owners to see the fruits of their labors daily.

Miss Emily Crawford Johnson, an elegant, courteous, gracious and charming lady, along with her mother, Ruth Monroe Gouverneur Johnson,

Houses built by Miss Emily Johnson and her mother. *Courtesy of Diversions Publications.*

decided at the beginning of the Depression in the early 1930s that banks were not a safe place. So they withdrew their money and hid it in the proverbial mattress in a bedroom in their Court Square home.

Miss Emily, as she was affectionately known, ran a small school in her home for many years, teaching the children of socially prominent families. She was so well respected as a teacher that few students ever uttered a harsh word about her.

A year or two after the notorious bank holiday, Miss Emily and her mother decided they wanted to put their money where they could see it every day without the difficulties of moving the furniture. They owned lots on Bentz Street facing Baker Park directly behind their home. With the help of friends in the building industry, they had three houses built there. Two were identical and attached. The third was separate but had the same floor plan: brick exterior walls, plaster walls and hardwood floors inside. Small kitchens but large living rooms. There was even a garage for each.

The story of these houses doesn't stop there, however. For all the years she owned the properties, Miss Emily kept a journal, recording every expenditure she made—from taxes to nails to plumbing repairs. On one occasion, she purchased a pound of nails at Quynn's Hardware on East Patrick Street. Every time she took a nail from that sack, she wrote in the journal where it was used and for what purpose. There are hundreds of like entries.

The houses may be the most visible sign of Miss Emily's life in Frederick, but by no means are they the sum total of her legacy. For those blessed by her friendship, she will forever be remembered as a true "lady" who passed though their life's journey. Fredericktonian Richard Lebherz, who was a student at her school, remembered upon her death in October 1984: "She was…a bulwark against the crass, the inelegant, the admirer of history and family. She was the rock against which little hands clung to for support upon entering the larger world that surrounded us…She made us realize that there was more to life than the living of it. For it was just as important how we beheld ourselves in life as how we lived it."

Miss Emily was extremely proud of her heritage, being the great-great-granddaughter of President James Monroe. She donated a small portrait of him to the National Portrait Gallery even though she could have received a small fortune for it. Even after she moved into a nursing home and had to downsize her belongings, she retained a desk given to President Monroe by President John Adams. It was her pride and joy.

As her days neared their end, a young admirer learned of her birthday and presented her with a dozen long-stemmed red roses as a small token of appreciation of her friendship through the years. Her smile that day lit her two small rooms in the nursing home. She was taken aback by the gesture—and she never forgot it either, frequently mentioning it to her niece and nephew.

With her passing, Frederick lost a giant in its history, remembered now only as the one who built those remarkable houses on Bentz Street. There was so much more to her.

WILLIAM OSBORN LEE JR.

Educator, Politician and Civil Rights Pioneer

A leader in the community, his church, as an educator and, most importantly, as a historian of the African American community, William Osborn Lee Jr. was highly influential in every aspect of his life.

Born on Frederick's West All Saints Street on May 7, 1928, he grew up in a segregated society and was denied access to local parks, service at local restaurants and the ability to try on clothes before purchasing them at local stores. He was sent to a school where only "his kind" went. But "Sonny," as

William Osborn Lee Jr. *Courtesy of Artist YEMI, from* Pillars of Frederick.

he was known to friends and family, made a difference, working quietly (most of the time) to change his community one day at a time, one person at a time.

He graduated in 1945 from Lincoln High School, the only high school for blacks in Frederick County at the time. After serving his country in the U.S. Navy for three years, he entered Howard University, earning a degree in physical education in 1954. He continued his studies at the University of Maryland and at Western Maryland College in Westminster.

Although he received job offers elsewhere, Lee was determined to come back to Frederick. His wife, Cynthia, a fellow Fredericktonian whom he'd married in 1948, objected. But he was determined. He became the coach and physical education teacher at his alma mater, a job he loved. With desegregation and the changing of Lincoln into an elementary school, Lee moved to West Frederick Junior High as an administrator. When the school became West Frederick Middle, he became its principal, a job from which he retired in 1983.

He wasn't done yet though. Not by a long shot. From 1986 to 1994, Lee served the City of Frederick as an alderman, the last four years as president pro tem. He influenced others to become involved in local politics and pushed a good friend, William Hall, into becoming an alderman, too.

His community involvements included his church, Asbury United Methodist, at which he served in every capacity except pastor. He also served on many boards of directors, including for Community Living, the Frederick County Public Libraries, the African American Resource Cultural and Heritage Organization, Fairview Cemetery, the Kiwanis Club of Frederick, Hospice of Frederick County, Goodwill Industries of the Monocacy Valley, Daybreak, the Police Athletic League, the United Way Review Board and the local branch of the NAACP.

During all his adult years in Frederick, Lee collected anything having to do with the history of African Americans in Frederick and Frederick County. Prodded by relatives and friends, he finally compiled a book titled *Bill Lee Remembers*, which was published by Diversions Publications in November 2003.

When it was discovered that the city he loved had, in the 1940s, bulldozed a mid-nineteenth-century cemetery for blacks, Lee actively participated in the project to restore Laboring Sons Cemetery between Fifth and Sixth Streets off Chapel Alley. On January 15, 2003, the Laboring Sons Memorial Ground was rededicated. It now includes a plaque listing the names of those buried there, but likely there were others whose names have been lost to history.

With the culmination of this project, Lee turned his attention to another: a museum of black history in Frederick. His dream hasn't come to fruition yet, but it remains a project in the back of the minds of many people, both black and white, as its creation would be a fitting tribute to this man who worked tirelessly to make Frederick a better place for all.

Lee was diagnosed with lung cancer just ten months before his death on January 11, 2004. But as a testament to his far-reaching influence, then Maryland Governor Robert L. Ehrlich Jr. and Lieutenant Governor Michael Steele made separate trips to Frederick to thank Lee for his contributions to his community, city, county and state.

Lee's wife, "Cynnie," survived her husband but a short time. A driving and calming influence in his life, she passed away on October 22, 2006. They are survived by two children: Vivian Marie Lee of Frederick and Hugh Andrew Lee of Bristow, Virginia.

Reprinted with permission from Pillars of Frederick, *2011, Great State Publishing LLC*

MARGARET BYRD RAWSON

Dyslexia's Grande Dame—A Window into the World

Few people who have chosen Frederick as their home have had the international influence of Margaret Byrd Rawson. Her efforts to identify people of all ages afflicted with dyslexia began in the 1930s and ended only upon her death in 2001.

As a young librarian at the School of Rose Valley near Philadelphia, she encountered a young man named Peter who was having great difficulty mastering the ability to read. She took it upon herself to uncover the problem. Through her painstaking efforts with Peter, and her future investigations, she became a world-renowned authority on dyslexia, traveling the United States as a lecturer, promoter, friend, teacher and founder of more than just a few schools dealing with this "disability."

Early on, she discovered the work of a "leading New York neurologist, Dr. Samuel Orton, who introduced her to dyslexia, the brain disorder that compromises the interpretation of special relationships among letters and words, transforming was into saw, for example." It was Dr. Orton, in collaboration with Anna Gillingham, who developed a means to teach children with this affliction. Margaret Rawson was the most outspoken supporter of their method for more than sixty years.

However, she never really thought of dyslexia as a disability. Rather, as Sara Engram wrote in *Marylanders of the Century*, "she aimed to show that labeling it simply as a 'disability'—rather than a form of intellectual diversity—reveals more about the limitations of traditional schooling than about the aptitudes of dyslexic youngsters."

To that end, she followed the careers of fifty-six students, twenty of whom were dyslexic, throughout their professional life. The result was a book, published in 1968, titled *Developmental Language Disability: Adult Accomplishments of Dyslexic Boys*. The work demonstrated that even children who suffer from this malady were just as successful as their counterparts in their chosen professions. She updated the book twenty years later, adding four chapters.

Mrs. Rawson and her husband, Alfred, moved to an old stone house on Rocky Springs Road near Frederick in 1946, a home they called "Foxes Spy." From 1947 to 1965, she was a professor of sociology at Hood College, developing a seminar on dyslexia.

After her husband's death in 1963, having raised two children, she devoted even more time to her "passion." She was the founder of the Jemicy School

Margaret Byrd Rawson. *Courtesy of Hood College.*

in Owings Mill (Maryland) in 1973, considered today to be a pioneering facility for Maryland youngsters. She also served on the advisory councils of several other schools devoted to dyslexic children.

She published nine books during her career and contributed numerous articles on the subject. She had a unique ability to communicate with professionals in the medical and education fields and easily translate those conversations and correspondence into language understood by others. It continued until her death on November 25, 2001. In her later years, she used modern technology to assist her in her own reading as macular degeneration robbed her of her eyesight.

Mrs. Rawson was born in Rome, Georgia, on June 30, 1899, and attended the local Friends School. She graduated Phi Beta Kappa from Swarthmore College in 1923 after a short career in publishing. She earned a master's degree from the University of Pennsylvania in 1940 and received two honorary degrees, from her undergraduate alma mater (1983) and from Hood College (1989). Other awards from the president of the United States, governors and educational facilities across the country are far too numerous to list.

But the rewards of her work she most appreciated were the letters and visits she received from those she tutored in person and through her lectures and writings. She cherished them.

Gamblers

CHARLES J. REMSBURG
A Gambling Man and His Casino

Charles J. Remsburg was among the first entrepreneurs in Frederick County to understand the profits to be made in raising goldfish. He also understood that politics and religion, the primary forms of entertainment in the eighteenth and nineteenth centuries, didn't provide the needed outlets many citizens demanded.

In the late 1890s, Braddock Heights was becoming the summer vacation spot for those trapped in the stifling heat of the metro areas. An observation tower, a bowling alley, a skating rink, a merry-go-round and a dance hall attracted hordes of people to the top of Braddock Mountain. Even the first stop on the Hagerstown and Frederick trolley system was at the resort.

So it was on September 9, 1908, that Remsburg opened his Lake View Casino near Lewistown. It offered dancing, bowling, pool, a box ball arena and a flickering motion-picture machine, all fueled by a modern acetylene light plant and a steam heating system. Thousands took the trolley, which eventually extended all the way to Gettysburg, getting off on the spur that Remsburg built to his resort. An extensive lake was constructed on the property to provide an outlet for swimmers and boaters. And a few years later, a thirty-six-room hotel—thirty with private bathrooms—opened, again to acclaim.

Lake View Hotel. *Courtesy of the Historical Society of Frederick County.*

But just twenty-one months later, a fire destroyed the casino. At about 3:30 a.m. on May 24, 1910, a "colored" man named Wolfe discovered a fire on the outside of the southwest corner of the casino and alerted authorities. A bucket brigade quickly formed, gathering water from the lake to be thrown on the fire. While efforts to save the casino were foiled, nearby buildings, including the hotel and the residence of the Remsburg family, were saved.

The casino fire was determined to be arson. The loss was estimated at $20,000, which included a storage shed containing about $500 in new and used roller skates and the usual supplies for such a facility, tobacco and sugar treats. Insurance covered less than half the loss.

Fate struck again four years later when another fire destroyed the hotel on June 16, 1914. Remsburg declined to rebuild.

Remsburg was born at the very beginning of the Civil War on April 24, 1861. After graduating from Eaton & Burnett's Business College in Baltimore, he returned to Lewistown and began farming. As early as 1890, he launched the business of raising goldfish. His grandchildren recall that some of his ponds were located in what is now Baker Park. There were also extensive breeding ponds in the Lewistown area, although it isn't clear just which ones belonged to Remsburg. At the height of his success in the business, Remsburg was shipping more than one million goldfish around the world.

The home he built adjacent to the casino and hotel was a Sears, Roebuck catalogue home and was shipped partway on the local trolley system to the site on which it now stands as the last remnant of the once flourishing resort.

Other family legends say that Remsburg visited the home of Mamie E. Pitzer just days after she was born. Commenting on the beauty of the baby, he reportedly said that she was so lovely that he would someday marry her. And thus it was that he waited until she grew up and, in fact, did marry her. They were the parents of two children: Charles Garnet Remsburg and Katherine (Kitty) Pitzer Remsburg, who married Dr. William Schnauffer, later owners of Spite House in Frederick.

Remsburg suffered a stroke in late September 1938 and died on October 6. After funeral services at his home at Lake View, he was buried at Utica Cemetery.

Note: There is some discrepancy as to the spelling of the last name of Mr. Remsburg. Williams's *History of Frederick County* spells it Ramsburg, but Mrs. Schnauffer always spelled her maiden name with an "e." Mr. Remsburg's funeral notice in the *Frederick News-Post* also spelled it with an "e."

Industrialists

JAMES H. GAMBRILL JR.
A Man for All Reasons

He was a man who was committed to his community, likely more than most men of his generation. His legacy stretches from post–Civil War Frederick County to the present day.

James H. Gambrill Jr. was born on March 9, 1866, in Baltimore and had eight siblings. He was raised in Frederick and received his education at the public schools and at the Frederick Academy. It is possible that his life could have taken a turn in the wrong direction when he was twenty-one, but he persevered and devoted the remainder of his life to the Frederick community.

James H. Gambrill Jr. *From Williams,* History of Frederick County.

James H. Gambrill Jr.

On the evening of December 10, 1887, young Gambrill, substituting as the guard for his father at the elder's Frederick Flouring Mill on South Carroll Street, shot and killed Nelson Stanton, whom he observed stealing coal from a pile in the mill's yard. He testified at a coroner's hearing the next day that the shooting was accidental, his gun firing as he chased Stanton up the hill toward South Street. The jury ruled in his favor, relying mostly on Gambrill's testimony.

It must have been a painful incident, for he left Frederick the next year and entered the mercantile business in Alabama, returning six years later to rejoin his father's business. For the next fifty-six years, he was involved in every aspect of life in the community.

He married Susan May Winebrenner, the daughter of another prominent Frederick family, on October 31, 1890. They were the parents of two children: James Henry Gambrill III and Susan May Gambrill, named for her mother, who died giving birth to her. Miss Gambrill grew up to marry Charles Lane, the brother of Maryland governor Preston Lane, and lived out her life on West Church Street in downtown Frederick. She was known as Mazie.

In 1898, Mr. Gambrill formed the Truckers Association of Frederick County, thus beginning a career devoted to the promotion of the agricultural heritage and benefits of this dominant industry. He was also an incorporator of the Frederick County Farmers Exchange in 1902. The company was later sold to Mr. Gambrill and D.W. Detrick, who had just completed construction of the Mountain City Mill. This building now houses the Delaplaine Visual Arts Center.

As a practical offshoot of his involvement in the milling business, Gambrill opened several baking enterprises, including G.L. Baking. This firm produced a "tough, flat, bland cracker" known as hardtack for shipment to American soldiers fighting in World War I. It provided needed nutrition and was easily carried by the soldiers.

On the occasion of Gambrill's seventieth birthday in 1936, a gala was thrown by his friends at the Francis Scott Key Hotel. Gambrill had been among those who financed and built the hotel. In news reports of the event, seven inches of one-column type was devoted to a list of the business and community organizations in which he was involved.

Gambrill was an ardent fisherman and hunter, and his devotion to the preservation of the natural beauty of Frederick County led to the naming of the forest at High Knob in his honor: Gambrill State Park.

When he turned eighty in 1946, his friends took up a collection for a special gift. The collected $100,000 was donated to Frederick City Hospital, and a wing, then under construction, was named for him.

Gambrill, who was named a Hood College trustee in 1916, was again honored when the college—in 1947—named its new gymnasium for him in recognition of his thirty years' service.

Although active in Democratic Party politics most of his adult life, he served only a single term in elective office, the Frederick Board of Aldermen (1907–10).

He died of a heart attack at a Baltimore hospital on October 17, 1951. After services at All Saints Episcopal Church, where he had served as vestryman for many years, he was buried at Mount Olivet Cemetery.

MANASSAS JACOB GROVE

Unparalleled Success in Numerous Fields of Endeavor

More than one hundred years after his death, the name M.J. Grove still resonates in Frederick County. He was a farmer, schoolteacher, merchandiser, entrepreneur, legislator, soldier and the most successful producer of lime for agriculture and the building trades in county history.

Manassas Jacob Grove was born in Middletown, Maryland, on February 17, 1824, the son of George W. and Elizabeth Biser Grove. His ancestors on the Grove side came to the Middletown Valley in 1770 with a group of Pennsylvania Germans who became prominent farmers. His mother's family owned several farms in the Broad Run section of the county.

Scholarly pursuits attracted M.J. Grove, but his lack of training in both Latin and Greek cut short his college ambitions. Instead, after he graduated from the Middletown Academy, school officials successfully enticed him into teaching. In ensuing years, he taught at Arnoldstown, Broad Run, the Union School near Jefferson and the Fink School near Middletown.

When he was twenty-two, the Mexican War erupted. Grove immediately enlisted in a local company of volunteers, but he was never called to actually fight in that conflict.

In 1851, Mr. Grove opened a mercantile business at Broad Run and soon after established another at Burkittsville. From 1852 to 1859, he was also the postmaster at the latter location.

Also in 1852, he married Susan Jarboe, whose ancestors were among the early settlers of Maryland, having arrived with the first Lord Baltimore into St. Mary's County. M.J. and Susan Grove were the parents of twelve children, five of whom died in infancy.

In the 1850s, Grove became increasingly interested in the emerging industry of generating lime for fertilizer by the burning of limestone, which seemed in an unending supply in the county. In 1859, he closed his two stores and bought a large track of land at Lime Kiln, just south of Frederick on the main line of the Baltimore and Ohio Railroad. A year later, after building a large home on the property, he moved there with his family.

The ensuing years saw his business expand to Frederick's East South Street (a quarry now owned by LaFarge North America, Inc.); a quarry at Stephens City, Virginia; a quarry at Buckeystown; and a coal and lime business in Washington, D.C. During the latter part of the nineteenth century, other uses for lime came into vogue, including lime for plastering and for brick and

Manassas Jacob Grove. *From Williams,* History of Frederick County.

other masonry production. At its heights, the company was operating twenty-five kilns to burn the limestone. Grove and his oldest son, William Jarboe, operated the company as M.J. Grove and Son from 1875 to 1889, when the M.J. Grove Lime Company was organized. As the years passed, all five of his sons became executives in the firm.

In 1887, Grove was elected to the Maryland House of Delegates as a Democrat, a position to which he was reelected in 1891.

Mr. Grove's wife, Susan, died in 1889. Two years later, he married Josepha Durr, the daughter of a prominent Virginia family. They did not have children.

In their later years, Mr. and Mrs. Grove traveled extensively. On visiting California, they called on G.K. Fitch, the owner of the *San Francisco Chronicle*, who had been a business partner of Mr. Grove's brother Martin Franklin Grove in the newspaper business. Martin Grove had borrowed money from his brother in 1849 to go to California, where he established the first newspaper in Sacramento.

On the evening of February 2, 1907, having worked a full day at his business, M.J. Grove suffered a fatal heart attack just fifteen days before his eighty-third birthday. He had been in good health until that day, according to local news accounts.

He was buried on February 6 in the cemetery of the Burkittsville Reformed Church following brief services at his Lime Kiln home. He was survived by his second wife, his five sons and his two daughters.

OUTERBRIDGE HORSEY II

Master Distiller

At a time when many Frederick County farms had stills for their own use and pleasure, Outerbridge Horsey II took the idea to a whole new level and produced some of the finest rye whiskey ever distilled in the United States.

Born into a prominent family on February 28, 1819, Horsey was the son of a U.S. senator of the same name, of Delaware, who married the daughter of Maryland's second governor, Thomas Sim Lee. Governor Lee succeeded Thomas Johnson in the post in 1779.

When he was nineteen years old, following his education in local schools and Mount Saint Mary's College, Horsey began the process of distilling whiskey, settling in short order on rye rather than whiskey produced from corn. His plant, on the Needwood property between Burkittsville and Brunswick, grew as his skill as a distiller advanced. But in 1862, as Civil War troops marched back and forth through Frederick County, his factory was destroyed and his product confiscated.

Wanting to learn more about how European manufacturers produced such smooth whiskeys, Horsey went to Scotland, Ireland and England, where, for three years, he studied their methods.

In 1865, he returned to Burkittsville and rebuilt his distillery, constructing a warehouse that would hold three thousand barrels of his "Very Fine Outerbridge Horsey's Rye Whiskey." His plant covered seven acres and eventually produced ten thousand barrels a year. But it wasn't cheap. He believed that the ocean voyage bringing European whiskey to America was what made it so smooth. Thus, he would ship his product to Baltimore and Washington, put it on a ship and sail it around Cape Horn to San Francisco. There, some of the whiskey was sold as "Golden Gate Rye" after another year in a warehouse. The rest was put on a ship for a return voyage to Burkittsville. Horsey also imported an Irish strain of rye for his sole use, adding again to the cost of producing his whiskey.

He proved his hypothesis correct. His rye was prized, and after the Volstead Act of 1919 found Needwood Distillery with thousands of bottles in storage, Frederick Countians were known to raid the warehouse, paying off guards assigned to guard the "booty."

But Outerbridge Horsey wasn't just a businessman. He delved into politics, having such men as John W. Baughman and Enoch Louis Lowe as mentors. He was for many years a member of the county's Democratic State Central

Outerbridge Horsey's distillery. *Courtesy of the Historical Society of Frederick County.*

Committee and once was cajoled into running for the state senate. He was defeated by Dr. Lewis H. Steiner, who later became the chief librarian of the Enoch Pratt Free Library in Baltimore.

"A man of dignified and commanding appearance," Horsey "easily won the respect and admiration of all with whom he came in contact," according to published reports at the time of his death on January 5, 1902. Just two weeks before his passing, he formed a stock company, naming his three sons to strategic positions with the firm.

His funeral was well attended and was conducted by a representative of James Cardinal Gibbons and the head of the Jesuit Novitiate in Frederick, which later that year moved to upstate New York. He was buried at St. Mary's Catholic Cemetery at Petersville.

His death was ill fated for the distillery, however. Not long after his passing, his sons switched to corn liquor, which never matched the popularity of their father's whiskey. The plant closed in 1919.

After Prohibition, other distillers copied the name, producing "Old Horsey Very Fine Rye Whiskey," "Old Horsey's Maryland Rye Whiskey" and "Old Horsey Rye Whiskey."

HENRY A. AND HENRY J. KNOTT

A Family Committed to Education

The Knott family, traced back to the early sixteenth century, has made an indelible mark on Frederick County, Baltimore City and County and particularly Mount Saint Mary's University and Catholic education across the state.

Henry A. Knott was born on the family farm in Urbana, Maryland, on September 25, 1878, the son of Frank and Sarah Margaret Mercer Knott. His father founded what became known as Knott and Geisbert in 1900, offering farm equipment and mechanical repairs. That firm closed in 2010.

Henry's early education was in local public schools. However, it was on the farm that he learned the value of a strong work ethic, which served him well and which he imparted to his children. As a farm boy, he developed great skill as a carpenter, and in the mid-1890s, he traveled to West Virginia, where he found work to hone his proficiency at his craft. It wasn't long before he was hired as an assistant superintendent for the James Stewart Co. of New York, which had large contracts in Baltimore. When the company was hired to build the Marlborough Apartments on Eutaw Place in 1902, Knott was made the general superintendent. And then the great fire of Baltimore in 1904 created building jobs for decades. In 1908, he formed his own company and built a reputation as the "Master Builder of Baltimore." The precept under which he worked was that "no job is so small that it should not be done as perfectly as humanly possible."

His company continually grew, and in 1917, he was awarded the contract to install all the woodwork in the Southern Hotel at Light and Redwood Streets. During World War I, he worked for the Steel Corporation and oversaw the construction of the officers' quarters at Edgewood Arsenal and the infantry barracks at Fort Meade. Following the war, he worked on numerous projects, including churches and other religious organizations.

His reputation was such that he was awarded his first contract in excess of $1 million. That was in 1929 and was for the construction of the Villa Maria Convalescent Home for Teaching Sisters of Notre Dame at Notch Cliff, just north of Baltimore. The building contained 141 rooms.

In the years leading up to his death on October 16, 1947, his company restored the dome of the State House in Annapolis and built the Church of Christ on University Parkway, the Church of Trinity Assembly on Harford Road and the Notre Dame Novitiate at Charles and Bellona Avenues in Towson.

Henry J. Knott. *Courtesy of the Knott family.*

Henry A. Knott married Martha Doyle in 1906, and they became the parents of six sons, all of whom survived him. One of them was Henry J. Knott, who formed Knott Masonry, which is still in business, now run by the third generation of the family.

It was the success of this firm that allowed Henry J. Knott and his wife, Marion—who had twelve children—to contribute more than $140 million to Roman Catholic institutions and hospitals. Mount Saint Mary's University in Emmitsburg was one of the beneficiaries of the Knott Foundation. Several buildings on the campus, including the Knott

Academic Center and the Knott Arena, were constructed with funds from this charitable group.

In a 1927 publication dedicated to inspire young men to emulate successful businesspeople in Maryland, it was written that Henry A. Knott "has achieved his success through the policy of being conscientious, truthful and particular in strictly keeping his promises. His advice…is to be faithful in the work [you] are doing and to leave nothing undone to satisfy customers."

Following a high requiem Mass at Baltimore's St. Ignatius Catholic Church conducted by his son, the Reverend Francis X. Knott SJ, he was buried at New Cathedral Cemetery.

LOUIS MCMURRAY
Entrepreneur, Canner and Inventor

Henry Ford is generally given credit for the invention of the assembly line. His product was a bit more expensive than that of one Louis McMurray, the father of the canning industry in Frederick. But McMurray preceded Ford in the use of the assembly line.

McMurray was born in western Baltimore County, now part of Carroll County, on February 23, 1823. His father, Samuel, gave up farming in 1840 and opened a restaurant in Baltimore, joined by his then seventeen-year-old son. When Samuel McMurray died in 1850, young Louis took over the business, knowing full well that serving food in a restaurant was not his calling.

During the year that he operated the restaurant, having learned through experience that fruits and vegetables and some seafood were not always available, Louis McMurray invented a process to hermetically seal cans. That discovery led eventually to one of the most beneficial and prosperous businesses in Frederick County's illustrious history.

In early 1852, McMurray began canning on a small scale in Baltimore. He continued for a few years before the Civil War erupted, and McMurray lost his southern and western customers. It led to his exploration of European and California markets for his canned goods.

After the war, McMurray expanded his business, but the failure of the peach crop in Maryland and Delaware in 1868 led him to southern Ohio, where he discovered "sweet corn." His taste buds told him there was a lucrative market for this field-grown delicacy. In early 1869, according to Jacob Engelbrecht's

Louis McMurray. *Courtesy of the Maryland Room of the C. Burr Artz Library.*

diary, McMurray bought three acres of ground from the Mantz family at the corner of South Bentz and West South Streets and began constructing his factory. Farmers with whom he had contracted to grow sweet corn were unfamiliar with the canning process, so they paid scant attention to the crop, and McMurray had little to show for his labors that year.

So he began buying farms all over Frederick County, mostly in Carrolton Manor, eventually owning more than 2,400 acres. Then he hired men to run them and cultivate—under his direction—the corn in a manner most beneficial to his business.

As the years passed, McMurray invented machines to make cans, another to seal them and several soldering devices. These allowed him to employ unskilled laborers rather than the journeymen needed when he first began canning.

At the height of his operations, he was able to produce more than 100,000 cans a day, and thus his use of the assembly line to perfection. According to published reports of the day, McMurray had sixty men pulling the ears in the field and loading twenty-five four-horse wagons. These teams arrived at the factory every ten minutes, and the sweet corn was sealed in the cans within a little more than one hour.

When the corn season ended in October, McMurray shifted production to huge warehouses on Cross Street in Baltimore, where he "packed" oysters, fresh from the Chesapeake Bay, using the processes he perfected in Frederick. His business boomed year round.

In October 1888, McMurray became seriously ill from an attack of dyspepsia, a malady from which he suffered for years. At the end of the month, he developed a painful sensation in his left ear. Doctors were unable to treat the illness with any success. On November 2, his conditioned worsened, and seven doctors were summoned to his side.

His wife, the former Jane Monica McDermott, rushed to their home on the "old Shell farm" east of Frederick from their Baltimore residence. Just before midnight on November 3, Louis McMurray passed into Frederick history. Funeral services were held in both Frederick and Baltimore prior to his burial in Greenmount Cemetery.

The only reminder of the great canning factory that stood on the north side of West South Street from Bentz almost to Ice Street is a little two-block roadway. It's called McMurray Street and is named for Louis McMurray.

Inventors

McClintock Young
Prolific Inventor

While still in grade school, McClintock Young developed a fire engine that would throw a stream of water more than forty feet—a remarkable feat considering this was in 1848. Before he retired sixty-two years later, he had in excess of one hundred patents and was largely responsible for one of the major manufacturing plants in Frederick.

Young was born in Washington, D.C., on June 25, 1836. His father was a great friend of Andrew Jackson and the grandson of Hugh Young, who fled his native Ireland after being implicated in the rebellion of 1798. His education was superior for the day, ending with a degree from St. John's College in Annapolis.

Young came to Frederick in 1856 and opened a foundry, likely at the southwest corner of South Street and present-day Broadway. He continued his penchant for invention, obtaining approximately thirty patents, including patents for steam engines, sawmills and sewing machines. His first profitable invention was a self-rake mechanism that he sold to the McCormick Harvester Company, which incorporated it in reaper machines for more than half a century. In 1870, he patented a match-making machine that he sold to the Diamond Match Company.

About 1886, Young, along with two Diamond executives, founded the Palmetto Brush Company, selling the idea of using palmetto leaves as brush

McClintock Young. *From Williams,* History of Frederick County.

bristles. Young's assignment was to develop a means to shred the leaves by machine. In 1887, he had made sufficient progress that the Ox Fibre Brush Company was formed and began operations at the old Page Foundry on West South Street.

In 1892, the brushes were selling so well that an ambitious plan for a new plant on East Church Street was developed. Eventually, it was decided to make brush handles as well as bristles. Before the middle of the twentieth century, the woodworking section of Ox Fibre rivaled most of the large furniture manufacturers in the amount of wood needed. Young completed his fully automated brush-making machine—from the shredding of the palmetto leaves to the insertion of the bristles into the handles—by 1898. It would also accommodate brushes of varying sizes with just a few adjustments. A single employee operating two of these machines at once could produce seventy thousand tufts for the brushes in a single day. During World War II, the plant produced twenty-five million brushes annually.

Throughout these years, though, Young didn't simply work on brush machines. He also patented a hinge-making machine that revolutionized that industry and invented a bicycle with pedals that powered the rear wheels, a great departure from the front-wheel pedals of the day.

Young was married on June 19, 1862, to Louisa Moberly, of New Market, who died in 1886. They had three daughters prior.

McClintock Young died on August 1, 1913, at his home at 118 North Court Street following a three-year illness. The cause of death was progressive palsy. He was buried at Mount Olivet Cemetery.

Journalists

Louis Victor Baughman
Dreams Unrealized

Few men have been as devoted to the Democratic Party as was Louis Victor Baughman. But his service fell victim to the whims of a powerful and unscrupulous U.S. senator who considered "promises [as] platforms made to get in [office], not to stand on."

"Vic" Baughman was born on April 11, 1845, the year his father John purchased the *Citizen*, which was among Frederick's leading weekly newspapers for nearly a century. Mary Jane, his mother, was the daughter of Baker Jamison, another prominent Marylander.

At age seventeen, he enlisted in the Confederate army, whose cause was supported by his father's newspaper. He was captured at the 1864 battle at Moorefield, West Virginia. His unit, part of the Rebel forces that had burned Chambersburg, was surprised by a stronger Union contingent. He was sent to Ohio's Camp Chase as a prisoner. He was part of a prisoner exchange in March 1865 and returned to Richmond, where he remained until the surrender at Appomattox.

After the war, he studied law and—for a time—was associated with his father's former partner, former Maryland governor Enoch Louis Lowe, in Brooklyn, New York. When his father died in 1872, Vic Baughman returned to Frederick and became the editor and publisher of the *Citizen*, ably assisted by his brothers.

But politics was his passion, and he worked every corner of Maryland to promote Democrats. It was usually behind the scenes, and his friendship with powerful Senator Arthur Poe Gorman gave him access to the inside track.

In 1888, a group of influential newspapermen met to discuss who should be the Democrats' candidate for governor in the upcoming election. The unanimous choice was L. Victor Baughman. A meeting with Senator Gorman was arranged, for his support was crucial. The senator sat in his Washington, D.C. office and listened patiently to the pleas and entreaties of the collected journalists. Then he went into a lengthy monologue, praising Colonel Baughman at every turn. But at the end, Gorman said that he had discussed the possibility of Baughman's candidacy with James Cardinal Gibbons, archbishop of the Baltimore Diocese. They had agreed, he said, that the time was not right to put a Roman Catholic in the governor's mansion. So Colonel Baughman was nominated for comptroller, a position to which he was elected twice. Despite this affront to his lifelong ambition, Baughman never once retreated from his support of Senator Gorman, who remained the most influential Democrat in Maryland until his death.

Aside from politics, Colonel Baughman and his wife, the former Helen Abell, daughter of A.S. Abell, the founder of the *Sun* of Baltimore, were noted statewide for the parties they hosted at their estate, Poplar Terrace. The farm was located on Shookstown Road between present-day Baughman's Lane and Montevue Lane. The Baughmans had a half-mile track on their manor, as the colonel was a noted horseman. Races were regularly held, and the accompanying parties were frequently lavish. He also maintained a prized "pack of hounds" for annual foxhunts.

In 1904, he announced that he would be a candidate for governor in 1907. Senator Gorman was in ill health and his influence diminished. The senator died on June 4, 1906. But Baughman's dream was never realized, as he succumbed to the lingering effects of a cold he caught while attending his stable of horses. His November 30, 1906 death was entirely unexpected.

While praises were lavish upon his passing, perhaps the greatest tribute came in T.J.C. Williams's *History of Frederick County*. It said: "His natural gifts and talents, his genial nature, warm heart, and engaging manners were such as to make the friends he had absolutely devoted to him...He believed in taking the public into his confidence and time and again he raised his voice in protest in the party councils against underhanded policies."

He is buried at St. John's Catholic Cemetery at Third and East Streets in Frederick.

L. Victor Baughman. *From Williams,* History of Frederick County.

FOLGER MCKINSEY

Bentztown Luminary

When just nineteen years old, Folger McKinsey came to Frederick as the city editor of the *Daily News*, hired away in 1886 from a small New Jersey newspaper by William T. Delaplaine. It was a fortuitous selection, as McKinsey spread the joy of Frederick wherever he went for the next sixty-four years.

As a friend of Walt Whitman, he developed a knack for poetry—which he wrote on his typewriter—and incorporated it in his writings as the first columnist for Baltimore's *Sun* newspaper from 1906 until illness incapacitated him in 1948.

He was born on August 29, 1866, in Elkton, Maryland, and received very little formal education. At age seventeen, he became the editor of the *Shore Gazette* in Ocean Beach, New Jersey. Delaplaine lured him away less than two years later.

One of the places McKinsey lived in Frederick was on West Patrick Street near Carroll Creek in an area known as Bentztown. Through the years, he developed characters to tell his stories in verse, including Freezer Fry, Uncle Billy Witmer, Aunt Petunia, Effie Zinglebower and Joey the Jail Poet, all residents of Pilduzer Park. Two volumes of his poems were published: *A Rose of the Old Regime* in 1907 and *Songs of the Daily Life* in 1911.

His stay in Frederick, which ended in 1898, was fortuitous for all present-day history buffs, as Thomas J.C. Williams asked him to research and write the local history from 1860 to 1910 for inclusion in his monumental work. And while Williams is credited as the author in conversation, McKinsey's name appears prominently on the title page of *History of Frederick County*.

Almost immediately after arriving in Frederick, he began writing articles calling for the erection of a suitable monument to Francis Scott Key, who at the time lay in an unpretentious grave in the family plot in Mount Olivet Cemetery. An organization had been formed ten years earlier but had lain dormant after an initial wellspring of enthusiasm. The revival of the Key Monument Association and the successful conclusion of its purpose with the erection of the glorious memorial in 1898 can be placed directly in the hands of Folger McKinsey. He remained the secretary of the group long after he accepted a position with a Baltimore newspaper that same year.

In 1906, he was hired by the *Sun* and shortly afterward began writing a five-day-a-week column called "Good Morning." His byline was always

Folger McKinsey. *From the collection of Mack Ridout.*

"The Bentztown Bard." It was a mainstay for the next forty-two years—until he became ill. The newspaper, however, because of popular demand, published repeats of his most acclaimed columns for another year.

Throughout the years following his departure from Frederick, McKinsey returned for special occasions to address various gatherings. He was among the prominent speakers at the 200th anniversary celebration of the founding of the city in 1945. And with each appearance, he wrote a poem to commemorate the event. Sadly, illness prevented his participation in the rededication of the Key monument in 1948.

One of his little-heralded accomplishments was as the winner of a contest to write an anthem for the city of Baltimore in 1915. His poem was among eight hundred entries in the competition initiated by Mayor James H. Preston. McKinsey was awarded the $250 prize. Music for it was written, and the anthem was sung at special events for years. Upon the return of the *Pride of Baltimore* from a winter cruise in 1980, Mayor William Donald Schaefer led a rousing chorus of the entire song, to the delight of the crowd.

Frederick County is still home to some of his descendants. He had married Fannie Dungan of Pennsylvania shortly before coming to town in 1886. Several of their children were born here.

Folger McKinsey died on July 22, 1950, at his home on the Magothy River in Anne Arundel County. He was buried in the churchyard of St. Margaret's Episcopal Church following services conducted by Bishop Noble C. Powell.

Lawyers

FRANCIS SCOTT KEY
The Tragedy of a Family Man

The author of our national anthem never really basked in the notoriety of his poetry, which, of course, his "Defence of Fort McHenry" really was. As an attorney who began his career in Frederick in 1800, he supported his family by becoming the U.S. attorney for the District of Columbia.

He found solace in his poetry and brought joy from sadness to many friends and family, especially to his wife, Polly. In his day, couples had many children, often losing several before they reached maturity. Of his eleven offspring, four died tragically and without warning.

Edward Lloyd Key was the first to perish. While living in Georgetown in the summer of 1822, Polly called Edward from his play and sent him off to school that July 8 afternoon, little knowing that it would be the last time she would see him. Her husband was on a business trip to Annapolis. After school, Edward and a friend decided to take a dip in the Potomac to relieve the oppressive heat of the day. Young Key swam out too far and was swept away. His companion didn't tell anyone until around 6:00 p.m., when Edward's brother John learned of the incident and rushed to the river. Edward's body was discovered hours later and carried home. He was eight years old. Both Francis and Polly had a premonition the day before that something was amiss, but neither expected it to be the loss of a child.

Francis Scott Key.
From the author's collection.

The Keys were quite proud of their children, especially Daniel Murray Key, who, although a troublesome youngster, was appointed to the Naval Academy. Daniel and John F. Sherburne, a fellow midshipman, had a disagreement while on a training cruise to the Mediterranean. Upon their return to Washington, the quarrel escalated, and Sherburne challenged Daniel to a duel on "the field of honor" near Bladensburg. They chose pistols. After the first shot missed both targets, Daniel Key demanded a second chance, and both men reloaded and fired. Daniel was struck in the chest and died twenty minutes later. It was near dusk on June 16, 1837.

Less than a year later, John Ross Key, third child and second son of Francis and Polly, and the brother who had led the search for Edward, was stricken with a mysterious illness and endured excruciating pain. It lasted but a few days, and John died May 21, 1837.

On January 11, 1843, Francis Scott Key died at the home of his daughter in Baltimore from complications of pleurisy. He was sixty-three.

Perhaps his death was a blessing, for Francis did not live to see his son Phillip Barton Key murdered by New York congressman Daniel Sickles in Lafayette Park on February 27, 1859. Phillip Key, the U.S. attorney for Washington, was having an affair with Sickles's wife, Teresa, who was seventeen years Sickles's junior. On that fateful day, Phillip Key stood in the park and waved his handkerchief at the Sickles home, which was his signal to Teresa to meet him at a prearranged location. Sickles, who at that moment was confronting his wife about the affair, saw Key's signal and became enraged. Grabbing his pistol, he ran across the street and shot Key several times. Key died on the spot—within view of the White House. The extraordinary part of this story is that Sickles was tried for murder and found innocent "by reason of temporary insanity," the first use of this defense in U.S. jurisprudence.

It is possible that Polly Key's death on May 18, 1859, was hastened by the murder of her son and the acquittal of Sickles on April 26.

While we look today to Francis Scott Key for patriotic inspiration, his life after he composed "The Star-Spangled Banner" was filled with tragedy.

LUTHER MARTIN

Lawyer and Contrarian

Perhaps in the history of Maryland there has not been a more precise, more eloquent or more astute legal mind than that of Luther Martin. His uncanny ability to recall details of legal precedents is unmatched by any lawyer who followed in his footsteps.

Born to humble beginnings on a New Jersey farm on February 20, 1748, Martin early on demonstrated a photographic memory, which allowed him to escape the hard life of a farmer and lead his chosen profession in its formative stages in establishing a new American legal system.

Martin left the farm in 1760 and enrolled at the College of New Jersey (now Princeton), where he remained for six years, earning high marks and establishing a reputation as a leader among men. In 1766, he chose to teach in Queenstown on Maryland's Eastern Shore, but after three

Luther Martin. *From Scharf,* History of Western Maryland.

years, he began the study of the law. The American Revolution was in its infancy, with citizens just beginning their open revolt against English taxation and domination.

When hostilities erupted in 1775, Martin was already well established as a promising legal mind, being heavily involved in the affairs of both Maryland and Virginia. Even at this early stage, he was known to be a thorn in the side of Thomas Jefferson, a role he cherished through the remainder of his life.

Although he joined the Continental army, he was recalled to Maryland in 1778 and became the state's attorney general, a post he would hold for the next thirty years. Perhaps his greatest accomplishment came in the Constitutional Convention in 1787 and thereafter. He rose to object to the abolition of states' rights. Although unsuccessful on many occasions in convincing his colleagues of the value of the states having greater power, many of his arguments as recorded are used today by attorneys arguing states' rights issues before the Supreme Court.

He was so beset with anger over the final draft of the U.S. Constitution that he refused to sign it for Maryland. He called the document, which he saw as the theft of individual freedoms and the ability of self-determination, "a stab in the back of the goddess of liberty."

Although he attained a national reputation in preventing the impeachment of Supreme Court justice Samuel Chase and for obtaining an acquittal of Aaron Burr, charged with treason in a plot with the Spanish government, he often took to drink, which dulled his senses and eventually led to a dramatic and swift decline in his health. One oft-told story relates that he promised a client that he would not drink during a trial. It dragged on longer than expected, and wanting to keep his word, he went to a bakery during a luncheon break and bought a loaf of bread. He then went to a tavern, bought a bottle of brandy, poured it over the loaf and ate it.

In 1819, while still attorney general, he suffered a series of strokes and basically became "non-compus mentus." The Maryland Assembly then passed a law requiring all members of the Maryland bar to pay a special fee that would be used to the benefit of Martin. Although rescinded a short time later, it is the only time in Maryland's history that any such law has been passed.

When Burr heard of Martin's condition, he came to the rescue, taking Martin under his wing and caring for him until his death on July 10, 1826, just six days after his nemesis Jefferson died.

Martin married Maria Cresap, the daughter of Michael Cresap, who led three hundred Frederick County sharpshooters on an eighteen-day march to Boston after the Battle of Bunker Hill. They wed on Christmas Day 1783. Although they had five children, only three girls survived to adulthood. Mrs. Martin died on November 2, 1796. Martin kept his promise to defend her father's reputation when allegations surfaced that questioned his patriotism.

JAMES MCSHERRY

Jurist Extraordinaire

It is revealing to research one who is the most prominent jurist in Maryland during the late nineteenth and early twentieth centuries. Yet little is revealed about his life outside the courtroom. Such a man was James McSherry, son of James McSherry and grandson of James McSherry. It is confusing because so many shared the same name and were distinguished only by their accomplishments and their birth and death dates.

James McSherry, the judge, was born on December 30, 1842, in Frederick, the son of a man who was lauded primarily for his literary works. He penned the third *History of Maryland*, markedly different from its two predecessors. This history compiled the important events in our state from 1634 to 1848 but told the story in simple narrative form. He also wrote frequently for Roman Catholic publications nationwide and penned a history of James I, who succeeded Elizabeth I of England in 1607.

Judge McSherry attained his early education at St. John's Literary Institute and matriculated at Mount Saint Mary's College in Emmitsburg. He had completed his studies but had not received his degree when the Civil War erupted. He was imprisoned for a short time at Fort McHenry in Baltimore because of his Southern sympathies, as were many other young Marylanders. He didn't go South during the war, instead studying law in his father's offices, and was admitted to the bar by Judge Madison Nelson in January 1864.

Early on, he garnered a reputation for hard work and a legal expertise rarely seen in the courts of Frederick County. He counseled most of the local businesses in one fashion or another, whether as a member of their boards of directors or in legal cases before the court.

Upon the death of Sixth Judicial Circuit judge John Ritchie in October 1887, McSherry was appointed to replace him by Governor Henry Lloyd and was unopposed in an election just one week later. This judgeship also carried with it a seat on the Maryland Court of Appeals. Judge McSherry was a tireless jurist, working long hours preparing written decisions, which were concise and full of easily understood language—even for the layman.

When Court of Appeals chief judge John Mitchell Robinson died unexpectedly in January 1896, Governor Lloyd Lowndes did not hesitate in naming his replacement. With written complimentary recommendations from his fellow judges in hand, Lowndes named McSherry to the post immediately.

Judge James McSherry. *From Williams,* History of Frederick County.

In the days when Judge McSherry served on the Court of Appeals, the court was in session during specified time periods. It was the practice of the judges to live together in the same house in Annapolis, sharing friendship and meals. So now, Judge McSherry moved to the head of the table and led the dinnertime discussions. Oh, to be a fly on the wall during meals in those days.

When he was first appointed to the court in 1887, Judge McSherry resigned most of his business connections, not wanting conflicts to cause him to recuse himself from important cases. He did, however, remain on the Board of Directors of the Citizens National Bank and the Mutual Insurance Company of Frederick.

In January 1907, Judge McSherry became ill with a malady never fully diagnosed by his physicians. He struggled with the illness, frequently seeming to be on the road to total recovery only to suffer setback after setback. He continued his appeals court work but curtailed all other labors.

On the morning of October 23, after a restful night during which one of his physicians remained at his side, he ate what was described as a hearty breakfast and retired to his living room to review some documents. At about 10:10 a.m., he threw up his hands and collapsed in his chair. His nurse, a Miss Nicodemus, was a few feet away but was unable to revive him.

Following services at St. John the Evangelist Roman Catholic Church, Judge McSherry was laid to rest in the church's cemetery. His wife and six children survived.

Thomas Stone

Signer of the Declaration of Independence

He was a Patriot, a man of strong beliefs who initially sided with those who felt negotiations with Great Britain was the true path to peace in the colonies. In the end, however, he was one of four men who signed the Declaration of Independence on behalf of Maryland.

Thomas Stone was born at Poynton Manor in Charles County in 1743, the actual date lost to history. His great-grandfather was William Stone, third governor of the Maryland palatinate. His family was especially prominent in our nation's early history, producing the aforementioned as well as a colonel in the Revolutionary War who later became governor of Maryland, an Episcopal bishop of the Maryland Diocese and a justice of the Court of Appeals.

After receiving a classical education with a Scottish tutor, Stone studied law in Annapolis with Thomas Johnson, later the state's first governor. After the Stamp Act was passed by Parliament, he traveled the state to acquire membership in local courts in a successful effort to avoid paying the required "fee." He settled in Frederick in 1764–65 to extend his legal training at a time when the Frederick County Court also served as the local government.

He married Margaret Brown, the daughter of another prominent Charles County family, sometime after he moved to Frederick. They remained here until 1770–71, returning to their native county, where they purchased an estate near Port Tobacco. They built a grand manor home they called Habre-de-Venture. That structure was partially destroyed by fire on New Year's Day 1977. (Although restored, it is now in private hands and is not opened to the public. It is, however, on the register of National Historic Landmarks.)

During the next sixteen years, Stone served in various capacities in government, from the state assembly as delegate and senator to a major role in the Continental Congress. He was among a handful of delegates who initially argued for negotiations with Great Britain but succumbed to the overwhelming arguments of his fellow Patriots. He voted for the resolution that states the colonies should be "free and independent states," although he and the other Maryland delegates were under instructions from the Maryland Assembly "to take no action for severing the connection of the province with the mother country."

The Continental Congress passed the Declaration of Independence in early July 1776, but until the restriction imposed by the assembly was

Thomas Stone. *Courtesy of the National Park Service.*

reversed, Stone did not sign it. Therefore, history records that the four Maryland delegates signed the document on August 2.

Stone was far from an eloquent speaker, preferring instead to lobby one-on-one with his fellow lawyers, delegates and senators. He once defended a fellow member of the Maryland Assembly who refused to pay the required poll tax. Among the lawyers opposing Stone in the case was Thomas Johnson. Stone, although "legally and morally correct" in his arguments, suffered for years from the public's outcry. It was this very case that determined his later stance of listening to the public's views before settling on his own course of action.

Though he was among those who wrote the Articles of Confederation and was elected to the Congress authorized to write our Constitution, his personal life interfered with the later obligation. His wife, Margaret, was in frail health following her inoculation for smallpox while residing with her husband in Philadelphia, where he was attending the Continental Congress. Her sudden death on June 1, 1787, sent Stone into great despair. His depression was so horrific that physicians prescribed an ocean voyage to Europe to renew his spirits. While awaiting passage in Alexandria, Virginia, on October 5, just four months after his wife passed away, Thomas Stone died at the age of forty-five, his place in American history forever ingrained. He was buried on his estate in Charles County.

Surviving were three children: Frederick; Margaret Stone Daniel; and Mildred, who married the brother of her sister's husband.

MILTON GEORGE URNER

Nestor of the Bar

Perhaps no other attorney in Frederick County's history—with the possible exception of Leo Weinberg—enjoyed the stellar reputation that befell Milton George Urner, whose long career led eventually to the creation of the Frederick County Bar Association. He was its first president.

Born on a farm near Libertytown on July 29, 1839, the son of Samuel and Susanna(h) Norris Urner, he was a descendant of Swiss immigrants who first settled in Chester County, Pennsylvania. His grandfather, Jonas Urner, "removed" to Maryland and farmed near Sam's Creek in present-day Carroll County and then in Frederick County.

Milton George Urner. *From Williams,* History of Frederick County.

After an early education in the county's public schools, Milton attended both Dickinson Seminary in Williamsport, Pennsylvania, and Freeland Seminary in Montgomery County, Pennsylvania. Ill health forced him to return to Frederick, where he taught school for two years (1856–57). In 1862, he began the study of law with Grayson Eichelberger, a fortuitous beginning to a long and distinguished career. He was admitted to the bar in 1863. Years later, Mr. Urner formed a law partnership with Edward S. Eichelberger, his preceptor's son.

He was elected state's attorney in 1871 by a substantial margin. In 1878, he was elected to the first of two terms in the U.S. House of Representatives, serving from 1879 to 1883. He was able, though usually assigned to

83

minor committees, to nevertheless distinguish himself as chairman of the Committee on Accounts in his second term.

Refusing to seek a third term, as was the case with so many "citizen politicians" of the day, he returned to Frederick and resumed his legal practice. But politics beckoned again, and in 1887, he was elected to the Maryland Senate. An appointment by President Benjamin Harrison as naval officer for the Port of Baltimore in 1890, which he discharged for four years, brought his political career to a close.

But Urner never lacked for something to do. His service to his community was so extensive that it may never be surpassed. For thirty years he was a director of Farmers and Mechanics National Bank before becoming the president of First National Bank of Mount Airy in 1904, which position he held until his death. The Mutual Fire Insurance Company, the Frederick Female Seminary, the Maryland Asylum for the Feeble Minded (Rosewood) and the Pennsylvania Railroad were beneficiaries of his expertise and immense popularity. He was a mason and an extremely active member of Calvary Methodist Episcopal Church, now Calvary United Methodist. He served this church as Sunday school superintendent for forty-seven consecutive years.

He was married on January 10, 1866, to Laura A. Hammond, the daughter of a Woodsboro physician. They were the parents of ten children, six of whom survived them. The best known was Hammond Urner, who became the chief judge of the Fifth Judicial Circuit Court and a judge on Maryland's Court of Appeals (1909–38). Mrs. Urner enjoyed a reputation as a poetess and composed a poem her husband insisted be read at his funeral. She died on July 31, 1923.

Though in his eighty-ninth year, Urner regularly attended sessions of the court in Frederick. On February 4, 1926, just three years after the formation of the local bar association, he attended court and greeted all with his normal cordial smile. He even sat through the assignments of cases by Judge Glenn H. Worthington, who was also a neighbor on Record Street just behind the courthouse. The next morning, he was taken sick, and his local physicians called in a specialist from Johns Hopkins in Baltimore. Urner developed pneumonia, and although lucid and able to carry on normal conversations, he slipped into a coma on February 8 and passed away the next morning.

He lay in state at his home, and after services at Calvary, he was buried at Mount Olivet Cemetery on February 11, 1926.

LEO WEINBERG

Country Lawyer, Gifted Orator

Perhaps in the history of Frederick County there has not been a more eloquent lawyer than Leo Weinberg, whose career spanned most of the first half of the twentieth century.

Born into one of Frederick's leading Jewish families, he discovered early that he loved English and classical language and its literature. Many were surprised by his ability to retain "word for word" whatever he read, demonstrating a photographic memory, which was to serve him well throughout his professional life.

His parents, Samuel and Amelia Lowenstein Weinberg, raised nine children at their Market Street residence and instilled in each of them a love for their faith and their community. Leo was next to the youngest, and while his sister Jeannette devoted her entire life to the local synagogue, Leo led the charge in the acquisition of a permanent home for the Beth Sholom Synagogue.

Upon his graduation from Boys High School in 1903, Weinberg entered Washington and Lee University, receiving a law degree in 1906. At the

Lexington, Virginia school, he excelled, even at this early age, in oratory, becoming the leading member of the Graham-Lee Literary Society.

He was admitted to the bar in 1907 and began his practice in association with Frank L. Stoner. The next year, Stoner invited Weinberg to join him in forming a new law practice. The invitation was quickly accepted, and while Stoner was already a well-established attorney, the new firm thrived, developing a special flair unmatched perhaps anywhere in Maryland.

Leo Weinberg as a young man. *From Williams,* History of Frederick County.

Leo Weinberg as a prominent attorney. *From* Tercentenary History of Maryland.

There is an old story about Weinberg that has stood the test of time. Other lawyers have related for years that whenever Weinberg was to argue a case before Maryland's Court of Appeals, they would close their offices and travel to Annapolis just for the opportunity to hear the eloquence with which he argued the case for his clients.

In Frederick, perhaps his most important case was in defense of Emory L. Coblentz, who faced several criminal and civil charges following the collapse of the Central Trust Bank and the closure of its fourteen offices. Coblentz was acquitted in every case, primarily through Weinberg's effective efforts.

But Leo Weinberg's lasting legacy in Frederick was the establishment of a synagogue. Surprisingly, Brunswick had its own Jewish worship center before Frederick. Weinberg was the keystone speaker at the groundbreaking for Beth Israel in 1917. At the close of Yom Kippur services that same year, Weinberg delivered an impassioned speech to the Frederick congregation starting a campaign for the establishment of a permanent home for the Frederick synagogue. His uncle, prominent local merchant David Lowenstein, immediately pledged $3,000. Lowenstein, sadly, did not live to see the fulfillment of this dream, as he died in 1919.

When the Elks Club opened its new facility on the north side of West Second Street, its old building became available, and Weinberg purchased it. It was located next door to his home, which he had built at the corner of Court and West Second Streets. He donated it to the congregation at the urging of the newly formed local chapter of the National Council of Jewish Women for the renovation to a synagogue. It was dedicated in 1923 and is still in use today, despite the construction of a larger and more modern Jewish Community Center on North Market Street.

In a footnote to his life, which ended suddenly on September 17, 1942, in a Philadelphia hospital, Weinberg had composed his own obituary. Its contents were never disputed. It read in part: "Thus death has closed a colorful, contradictory career. He was indeed intolerant of opposition, yet he identified himself with a profession in which he was bound to be opposed. He advocated law and the social standards and conventions arising out of them. Yet he violated them. He knew all of the thrills of ecstasy and felt all of the pangs of misery. He was either at the apex of glory or in the abyss of despair."

Leo Weinberg was buried in the Baltimore Hebrew Friendship Cemetery.

GLENN H. WORTHINGTON

Educator, Jurist and Historian

As a small boy on July 9, 1864, Glenn H. Worthington was witness to history as the Battle of Monocacy unfolded on his parents' farm at Frederick Junction. He stood on a box and viewed the action through a basement window, as did other members of his family. More than sixty years later, he published a compelling book about that fight, in which he put forth the proposition that had not General Lew Wallace and 7,500 Union soldiers engaged 17,000 Confederate troops under the command of General Jubal A. Early, the nation's capital may have fallen into Rebel hands. Although General Wallace was greatly outnumbered, his actions gave other Union

Top: Judge Glenn H. Worthington. *From Williams,* History of Frederick County.

Bottom: Judge Glenn H. Worthington. *From the author's collection.*

forces the time necessary to return from Richmond to reinforce Washington. It is a hypothesis that has stood the test of time.

It may seem like a small contribution to Frederick County's history, but Glenn Worthington's book was but a footnote in the record of his accomplishments.

After his local schooling and a sojourn in Chicago, where he worked in the wholesale business and insurance, he returned to Frederick to study law with preeminent attorney Milton G. Urner, who was the founding president of the Frederick County Bar Association. To support himself during those years, Worthington taught school in Walkersville. Desiring to receive a course of lectures in the law, he secured a teaching position in Baltimore as an adjunct to his attendance at the University of Maryland School of Law.

He returned to Frederick after graduating in May 1887, and in early 1888, on the recommendation of Daniel T. Lakin, Frederick County's first school "superintendent," he succeeded Lakin. During his four years in the position, the county opened its first high school in Middletown, adopted a prescribed course of study for all classes and standardized teacher qualifications, and Worthington personally prepared examinations for all grades, passage of which was required for promotion to the next level.

He resigned as school examiner in 1892 to devote his full attention to his law practice. On November 16, 1907, after serving four years as the county's state's attorney, he was appointed to succeed James McSherry as chief judge of the Sixth Judicial Circuit Court, which served both Frederick and Montgomery Counties. Two years later, he was defeated at the polls by Hammond Urner, and he returned to private practice.

In 1912, he was elected to a full fifteen-year term on that court as an associate and served with remarkable distinction. Upon his retirement in 1927, many in the local legal community complimented him on his "fairness, diligence, ability and impartiality" in the performance of his duties as a judge.

Instead of returning full time to the practice of law, Judge Worthington devoted himself—with the same passion with which he attacked his judicial work—to researching the Battle of Monocacy. He spent countless days in military archives in Baltimore and Washington, reading every scrap of paper he could locate dealing with that engagement. It took five years, but in 1932, his book *Fighting for Time* was published and received glowing reviews across the country. It was a crowning achievement of a life devoted to his community.

Judge Worthington was a mason and served in numerous positions in the Columbia Lodge, No. 58, A.F. and A. Masons. But the Knights of Pythias, where he was a member for more than forty years, was his first love.

He also served as president of the Historical Society of Frederick County and was a member of the United Fire Company.

Judge Worthington died on August 7, 1934, after an illness of about a month. He lay in state at his home at the corner of West Second and Record Streets. He was buried at Mount Olivet Cemetery after services at All Saints Episcopal Church, where he had served on the vestry for many years. The Reverend Douglass Hooff officiated.

He was survived by his wife, the former Julia Alvey, and five children.

Merchants

CASPER EZRA CLINE
Entrepreneurial Prodigy to Frederick's Leading Citizen

Throughout Frederick's history, outstanding men of accomplishment rose to the occasion and planted the seeds that grew into a city known and loved by anyone who lived here—or just visited.

Casper Ezra Cline made his mark early in life, graduating from the old Frederick Academy at fourteen. He immediately got a job as delivery clerk for Charles E. Thomas, who operated a carpet store on North Market Street. To everyone's surprise, upon the death of Mr. Thomas, young Cline bought the business, his mother signing the legal papers because he was still a "juvenile." It was 1888.

Casper Ezra Cline. *From* Tercentenary History of Maryland.

Casper Ezra Cline (left) and his father, Nicholas O. Cline. *Courtesy of the Cline family.*

Born on July 31, 1872, on the Locust Level Farm south of town, he was the son of Nicholas O. and Annie A. Michael Cline. The thought of leaving this community never entered his mind. Until the 1970s, the Cline name was associated with a thriving community, delivering quality furniture from several locations near the Square Corner. But that isn't even a small part of Casper Cline's investments in Frederick.

When Marshall L. Etchison died in 1914, Cline purchased his funeral business, leaving it in the hands of his store manager, William Griffin, while he went to school to learn the embalming trade. The Cline Funeral Home, which operated from 8 East Patrick Street, having been in business for forty-four years, was sold to Robert E. Dailey in 1958.

Always thinking of expanding his business, Cline moved several times before ending up at 10–12 South Market Street. At one time, his furniture store was located on the southwest corner of Market and Patrick Streets.

In 1914, he led the formation of Commercial State Bank, becoming the institution's first president. He remodeled the property at 1 South Market Street into a bank and moved across the street. The bank fell victim to the bank holiday in 1933.

After moving into the L-shaped building (8 East Patrick Street connecting with 10–12 South Market Street), Cline became the first local merchandiser to offer a motorized delivery vehicle, the second to install an elevator, the second to add electricity to a store and the first with a motorized hearse, which doubled as an ambulance. In 1940, Mr. Cline Furniture was the oldest continuous business to advertise in the *News* and the *Frederick Post.*

Commercial enterprises were not his only interests. When Frederick's Board of Trade was issued the first charter of the fledgling national Chamber of Commerce, Cline was among the original members who made the transition and was the first president of the new organization.

His compelling and abiding influence on the youth of the community was demonstrated prominently when he succeeded Dr. Joseph H. Apple Jr. as president of the Young Men's Christian Association.

As Braddock Heights flourished as an amusement park and vacation destination, Mr. and Mrs. Cline lived there during the summers for many years.

Because of his prominence in the community, he was invited to serve other local institutions, including the Mutual Insurance Company and the Frederick City Hospital. He was a member of the Frederick Rotary Club and the state and national funeral directors' associations. He was also a member of Calvary Methodist Church, serving more than twenty-five years as Sunday school superintendent.

Cline was married on September 5, 1893, to Minerva I. Frost. They were the parents of five daughters and a son, Casper E. Cline Jr., who joined his father's furniture and undertaking business in 1929. On April 7, 1947, following six months of ill health, Cline succumbed to a cerebral hemorrhage at the home of his daughter on Rockwell Terrace. He was buried two days later at Mount Olivet Cemetery. Mrs. Cline predeceased him in 1941.

Charles Baltzell "Broadway" Rouss

Colossus of New York

Frederick County is justly proud of its natives who have gone elsewhere to make a name for themselves: Clair McCardell, Winfield Scott Schley, Bishop Robert R. Roberts and the Nelsons, Roger and John, among others. A name perhaps unfamiliar to just about everyone is a man born on February 11, 1836, in Woodsboro.

Charles Baltzell Rouss came into this world in humble beginnings and left a legacy of philanthropy, including New York's Central Park, firehouses in Virginia, a Confederate States Archives in Richmond, a science building at the University of Virginia and Winchester, Virginia, where his mercantile life had its beginning when he was just fifteen. He was a man determined to succeed, though failure struck him often.

Charley Rouss quit school and went to work in Jacob Senseney's Winchester store at one dollar a week. He learned quickly the values and business acumen that would serve him well for nearly half a century. He opened his own store at eighteen with just $500, which he saved while working for Senseney.

Although everyone thought him too busy to have a social life, on August 26, 1858, he married Margaret Keenan, daughter of a prominent Winchester family, described in local papers at the time as "one of the most beautiful and well-educated belles."

Shortly after the Civil War erupted, he moved his business to Richmond, where he became a blockade runner, selling merchandise at what it cost him. The war took its toll, and it wasn't long before he was broke. He enlisted in the Confederate army in 1864 and was at Appomattox for the surrender.

A year after the war, Charley Rouss went to New York to gain fame and fortune. He was successful beyond his dreams, although initially he slept on park benches and ate at soup kitchens. He struggled mightily in those early years, even spending some time in debtors' prison. The mid-1870s were a disaster. In 1876, he found himself broke again, as were many others following the recession of 1873.

He never abandoned the principles he learned in Winchester, and eventually success returned. After changing his middle name to Broadway, he put his full name across the top of his store. He became known as Broadway Rouss, but he remained Charley to his friends.

Charles Baltzell Rouss. *Courtesy of Stewart Bell Jr. Archives, Handley Regional Library, Winchester, Virginia.*

For the next quarter century, he was mentioned with the Vanderbilts, the Rockefellers and the Woolworths. By 1880, he was a millionaire and remained so until his death.

His philanthropy knew few bounds. In New York, he donated a statue of George Washington and General Lafayette, which still stands in Lafayette Square. In Winchester, he had an iron fence installed around Mount Hebron Cemetery, along with a huge mausoleum for his family and a chapel.

When he donated a new firehouse in Winchester, the company changed its name to the Charley Rouss Fire Co. #2. He provided the funds for an upgrade of Winchester's water system and the money necessary to build that city's seat of government, known even today as Rouss City Hall. Inside the front door is a life-sized statue of him.

Although blind most of the last decade of his life, Charley Rouss still participated in Winchester events, especially annual parades.

When he died on March 3, 1902, Winchester closed down. Everyone in town wanted to pay their respects to this Colossus of New York who sprang up among them. Although there was a blinding snowstorm the day of his funeral, most Winchester citizens attended.

Frederick County, Maryland, although not a part of Rouss's life after 1841, was for his daughter Virginia Duane Rouss, who married Dr. Hopkins Gibson, the son of a Frederick physician. It was her second marriage, the first being to a clerk in Rouss's New York store. She and her husband moved to Frederick in 1932. She died on April 28, 1949, the last of "Broadway's" immediate family. She was buried in Shepherdstown, West Virginia. Her only survivor was a daughter from her first marriage.

Military Men

Lawrence Everhart
Heroic Soldier, Patriot, Minister

Perhaps in local history no single individual has received more recognition for his exploits in defense of our country than Lawrence Everhart. He was born on May 6, 1755, in the small village of Hessheim, Germany. He was baptized on May 8, 1755, in the Reformed Church there. His name then was Johannes Lorentz Everhardt. When he came to this country, arriving in Philadelphia in 1764, he was listed as Lawrence Everhart by immigration officials. The family immigrated to the Middletown Valley.

Lawrence was "tall of stature, and of powerful, brawny limbs, capable of enduring fatigue and hardship; of noble, manly countenance, and an eye beaming with the lustre of genuine courage; with a heart beating high and strong to redress the wrongs of his country."

On August 1, 1776, he enlisted in the Continental army's "Flying Camp" under the command of Captain Jacob Goode. His first engagement was less than a month later, when he participated in a battle on Long Island and the Battle of White Plains and retreated with the army to Fishkill. When his original enlistment expired, Everhart refused to be mustered out and remained with General George Washington during the retreat through New Jersey. In the spring of 1777, he returned home, but the patriotic fervor that burned brightly within him spurred him to reenlist.

Lawrence Everhart. *Courtesy of the Historical Society of Frederick County.*

This time he joined Colonel William Washington's cavalry for the southern campaign. He remained with Washington and was involved in a series of battles and skirmishes in which the colonial army was frequently defeated by the British under an officer named Banastre Tarleton.

It was at the Battle of Cowpens on January 17, 1781, that Everhart achieved immortality. Washington sent men to reconnoiter enemy positions. Everhart, who was now a sergeant, and his command were discovered and overtaken by the British. He was wounded and captured when his horse was shot from beneath him. It is said that Tarleton came to Everhart and asked if his forces would be attacked that day. Everhart replied that he would be if Washington could keep two hundred men together. Tarleton indicated that he would defeat the colonials, to which Everhart replied, "I hope to God it will be another Tarleton defeat." To which Tarleton said, "I am Colonel Tarleton, sir!" "And I am Sergeant Everhart, sir."

As the Battle of Cowpens proceeded, Everhart—as a prisoner—was taken to the field, and when it became obvious that the British would lose, he was shot over his eye. The wound was not serious. He rejoined the victorious colonials, and when he pointed out to Lieutenant James Simon just which British soldier had shot him, Simon shot him and gave his horse to Everhart.

In his eagerness to pursue the retreating British, Washington found himself in front of his troops. British soldiers wheeled around and charged him. As one of them swung his sword at Washington, Everhart intercepted it with his own blade. Later, Tarleton thrust his sword at Washington again and it was parried. The officer took a few steps backward and fired his pistol at Washington, who was struck in the knee. After the battle was won, Washington sent Everhart to the rear to have his severe wounds treated. Everhart saw little action after that, but he was at Yorktown when Cornwallis surrendered.

Everhart returned to the Middletown Valley. He had married Ann Mary Beckenbaugh during the war. They were the parents of nine children. There are records that in 1799, Colonel Washington visited Middletown, and when the old compatriots spied each other, they ran into each other's arms and embraced for a long time with tears streaming down their faces.

Between the end of the war and 1808, little is known of Everhart's activities. We know that he was ordained a Methodist minister in 1808 by Bishop Francis Asbury and served several churches, both Methodist and Reformed, until his death in 1840. We also know that he met General Lafayette at Jug Bridge in 1824 and escorted the Frenchman to town for lavish ceremonies. Everhart had carried a wounded Lafayette from the field at the Battle of Brandywine near Philadelphia in September 1777.

On August 1, 1840, while on his way to Hagerstown to meet with William Henry Harrison, who was campaigning for president, Everhart suffered a stroke in Boonsboro. He returned to his home on the Catoctin Creek just west of Middletown, where he died a few hours later. He was buried with full military honors in the Methodist Cemetery, now part of Middletown's Lutheran Cemetery.

David Geisinger

Hero on the High Seas

Francis Scott Key, author of our national anthem, isn't the only hero of the War of 1812 with a direct connection to Frederick, although it is likely few have ever heard of David Geisinger, who served his country for more than fifty years in the navy. His career spanned several armed conflicts and landed him in the forefront of negotiations to open trade in the Far East.

Geisinger was born on December 28, 1790, in Frederick, the first of eleven children of Frantz and Sarah Levi Geisinger. The family later moved to the Middletown Valley.

The call of the sea must have been strong, for as soon as he was old enough, Geisinger sought appointment as a midshipman. He got his wish in November 1809. His first assignment was aboard the brig *Siren*. In May 1810, he boarded the *Constellation*, and when the United States declared war on England the next month, the ship was blockaded in Norfolk.

In the spring of 1814, he was assigned to a new sloop of war, christened the *Wasp*. It was built in Newburyport, Massachusetts. When it sailed on May 1 under the command of Johnston Blakesley, Geisinger was still a midshipman. In short order, he commanded the respect and admiration of the captain.

Within weeks of arriving in the English Channel, with orders to disrupt British shipping, the *Wasp* had captured or destroyed three ships. On June 28, it spied the HMS *Reindeer*, and a deadly encounter ensued. During the engagement, Geisinger was the first to board the enemy ship, drawing attention to his gallantry.

David Geisinger. *Courtesy of the United States Naval Academy.*

The *Wasp* was severely damaged in the incident and put into L'Orient, France, for repairs. It sailed again on August 27 and within days captured or sank several enemy vessels, even attacking a convoy protected by a lead warship. On September 21, sailing near the Azores, it came upon a British brig, the *Atalanta*, which quickly fell to superior power. The spoils of this victory were considered far too valuable, so Commander Blakesley, recalling vividly Midshipman Geisinger's heroic actions in the *Reindeer* encounter, placed him in charge of the *Atalanta* with orders to sail it to Savannah, Georgia. The *Wasp* and Commander Blakeley were never heard from again. It is presumed that both were lost in a storm at sea. Less than a month after arriving in Savannah, Geisinger was promoted to lieutenant.

Over the next several years, the young officer continued to distinguish himself. One of his postings was to Boston, where he met and married Catherine Russell Pearce, with whom he had four children. The first was Johnston Blakesley Geisinger, named for the lost commander of the *Wasp*.

In 1829, at about the same time that he was promoted to commander, Geisinger was honored by a resolution of the Maryland General Assembly in recognition of his wartime accomplishments.

But the best was yet to come for Geisinger. In 1832, he was given the command of the *Peacock* and ordered to transport Diplomat Edmund Roberts to Cochin China (what we now call Vietnam) and Siam to negotiate trade agreements. After failed negotiations in Saigon, Geisinger sailed to Bangkok, where he and Roberts met with great success. On March 20, 1833, they obtained the first commercial trade agreement with the King of Siam. With the treaty in hand, Geisinger sailed to Arabia. Again, with little coaxing, an agreement with Arabia was negotiated. The *Peacock* then returned to New York.

From 1836 until his retirement, Geisinger seldom went to sea. His last assignment was as commander of the United States Naval Asylum in Philadelphia. He was placed on the Reserve List in 1855, where he remained until his death on March 5, 1860.

David Geisinger remains among the Frederick Countians with exceptional military careers. He is, however, one of the very few who distinguished themselves on the high seas.

BRADLEY TYLER JOHNSON

Lawyer, Public Servant and Soldier

He was a rising political star in Frederick County and the state of Maryland when the Civil War erupted in April 1861. He was convinced of the rightness of the Southern cause, and thus he took his energies and abilities into another world, one in which he climbed the ranks in the Confederate army, eventually becoming—after the war—a Virginia state senator.

Bradley Tyler Johnson was born on September 29, 1829, in Frederick, the son of Charles Worthington Johnson and grandson of Baker Johnson, Governor Thomas Johnson's brother. He attended local schools and later attended Princeton University, receiving his degree in 1849. He then matriculated at Harvard Law School, receiving his degree in 1851. He returned to his hometown and put his name on the ballot for state's attorney. To no one's surprise, he was elected.

Johnson ran for state comptroller in 1857 but was defeated. He practiced law and remained involved in local politics, always espousing the Southern cause as the rhetoric escalated leading up to the war. When fighting erupted after Fort Sumter, Johnson gathered a company of like-minded men and marched to Point of Rocks. His men were poorly equipped and ill prepared

Bradley T. Johnson. *Courtesy of Artist YEMI, from* Pillars of Frederick.

for the conflicts to come. His wife, the daughter of a prominent North Carolina judge, offered to seek assistance in her home state. Ten days after departing the encampment, she returned with "500 Mississippi rifles," provisions enough to sustain the company for some time and enough uniforms for more than three hundred men. Shortly afterward, Johnson and his men joined forces with soldiers waiting at Harpers Ferry to form the First Maryland Line. He was named a major, third in command.

Throughout the war, no officer was engaged in more action than was Johnson. Principal battles in which he participated included both Battles of Manassas, several engagements surrounding Richmond, the Shenandoah Valley campaign of Stonewall Jackson and Gettysburg, following which he coordinated the retreat to Virginia.

For a time, he was the provost marshal in Frederick when Confederates held the town. He was promoted to brigadier general in 1864.

Following his brilliant career in service to the Confederacy, Johnson settled in Richmond, restarting his legal career. He was elected to the Richmond City Council and eventually the Virginia State Senate. His specialty was constitutional law, and he wrote several pieces of legislation that had a profound effect on the recovery of his adopted state from the ravages of the war. Perhaps the most far-reaching and important law he authored was one that established a "new, complete and just registration for voters" of Virginia.

In 1878, Johnson moved to Baltimore, setting up a law partnership with John P. Poe, who was married to Johnson's cousin. During these years, he was the leader of the Society of the Army and Navy of the Confederate States, which eventually established a home for Confederate veterans in Pikesville. When his partnership with Poe dissolved, Johnson practiced law with his son Bradley S. Johnson in both Baltimore and Virginia.

After retiring, Johnson devoted his time to literary pursuits and wrote several books, including a biography of George Washington, a Confederate history of Maryland and a memorial to General Joseph H. Johnston, under whom he served during the war.

A short time before the Spanish-American War, Johnson went to Cuba as a newspaper correspondent, submitting numerous articles about life on that island.

His wife, Jane Claudia Saunders Johnson, died on December 31, 1899, and was buried in the Loudon Park Cemetery near the Confederate Soldiers Home in Pikesville.

General Johnson died on October 5, 1903, at the home of his son in Goochland County, Virginia. After a memorial service in Richmond, he was taken to Baltimore, where services were held at Christ Episcopal Church. He was interred next to his wife at Loudon Park.

Reprinted with permission from Pillars of Frederick, *2011, Great State Publishing LLC*

WINFIELD SCOTT SCHLEY

The Hero of Santiago

The name Schley is revered in Frederick County. Many notables have borne that surname, including John Thomas Schley, who immigrated to the colonies from Germany in 1739 and is credited with building the first house in the new Frederick Towne in 1746. A direct descendant, also named John Thomas, was a prominent lawyer, farmer and merchant. But his most notable accomplishment remembered today is that he was the father of Winfield Scott Schley, who was born on October 9, 1839, just one hundred years after the family arrived in America.

Admiral Winfield
Scott Schley. *From
Williams,* History of
Frederick County.

The young Schley was named after General Winfield Scott, who, at the time, was perhaps America's greatest living soldier, with the possible exception of William Henry Harrison, "Old Tippecanoe." An apocryphal story, floated for many years, claimed that Schley was named after the general laid the cornerstone of the "new Evangelical Reformed Church" on West Church Street on June 12, 1848. General Scott was in Frederick to attend a "court of inquiry."

The young Schley, favored by his birth into a prosperous family, received the best education available in Frederick and entered the United States Naval Academy in 1856. Upon graduation four years later, he was assigned to the frigate *Niagara,* carrying Far Eastern diplomats back to their homelands. Just two years after his graduation, he was made a lieutenant and saw action in the Mississippi River campaigns of 1862–63.

After the Civil War, he was again promoted and was assigned to the Naval Academy as an instructor. After three years, he went to sea again, serving in the Far East before he returned for another stint at Annapolis.

In 1884, after two unsuccessful efforts to rescue Lieutenant Adolphus Greeley's North Pole expedition, Schley agreed to lead another attempt. It was this successful mission that first brought Schley to national attention. He was hailed as a hero and received accolades from both the Maryland legislature and the Massachusetts Humane Society.

But Schley's real triumph came in 1898, when he commanded a squadron of American ships in the waters off Cuba near the start of the Spanish-American War. William T. Sampson was his superior officer on July 3, but Sampson left the fleet in Schley's custody to confer with army officers about tactics. It just so happened that the Spanish fleet, anchored in Santiago harbor, decided to make for the open sea and ran directly into Schley's forces. All four of the Spanish ships ran aground under heavy bombardment from the American vessels, made up mostly of converted pleasure ships. Schley was again touted, this time as the "Hero of Santiago." He made a whirlwind tour of major cities, where he received many honors. He was promoted to rear admiral by the president. When others claimed that Schley didn't deserve "hero" status, he made his now famous remark, "There is enough glory to go around."

In 1901, while at home attending to his son, who had been stricken with food poisoning, a textbook was published claiming Schley "dawdled throughout the campaign and had cravenly sheered away from the [Spanish] flagship when it made an attempt to ram" Schley's command vessel. Schley quickly demanded a "court of inquiry," which in the end criticized him but said he had acted properly at Santiago.

It wasn't long after that that Schley retired from the navy and drifted into anonymity, reflected greatly when, on October 2, 1911, he suffered a fatal heart attack on the streets of New York City. As he lay dying on the sidewalk, passersby didn't recognize him. How fleeting is fame?

He was buried in Washington, D.C. He was survived by his wife, the former Anna Rebecca Franklin, and three sons.

Russell Randolph Waesche

From Landlocked to the High Seas

Frederick Countians have excelled in many fields of endeavor during the past 250-plus years, but perhaps none achieved the success of Russell Randolph Waesche, who was born on Park Lane in Thurmont, Maryland, on January 6, 1886, the son of Mr. and Mrs. L.R. Waesche.

A quiet, unassuming man, Waesche rose through the ranks to become the longest-serving commandant in the history of the United States Coast Guard, appointed by President Franklin D. Roosevelt in June 1936 and retiring on January 1, 1946. His record still stands.

After attending Thurmont public schools, he enrolled at Purdue University. During his one year there, he passed an admission exam for what was then called the Revenue Cutter School of Instruction. This institution, then located at Curtis Bay near Baltimore, became the Coast Guard Academy in 1915. Waesche enrolled in 1904 and graduated in 1906.

During the next thirty years, he commanded the respect of his men and his superiors, always adding to the operations of the Coast Guard through careful and thoughtful study of just what would benefit those who served in his branch of the armed forces. He was assigned to ships in the Great Lakes, the Atlantic and Pacific Oceans and the Bering Sea. In 1915, he returned to the academy, then located at New London, Connecticut, and remained there until the end of World War I, after which he returned to sea duty.

Throughout his service, Waesche sought to improve the Coast Guard. He originated the service's Institute and Correspondence School for warrant officers and enlisted personnel. It was at his direction that a plan for the reorganization of the Coast Guard field forces was adopted in 1932. And even before he became commandant, he helped develop the government's plans to integrate the Coast Guard, a part of the Treasury Department, into the U.S. Navy in case of war.

In June 1936, President Roosevelt named him commandant, a post to which he was reappointed twice. During Waesche's tenure, the small, peacetime force of 15,000 men expanded to 160,000, commanding 750 cutters, 3,500 miscellaneous smaller craft, 290 navy vessels and 255 army vessels. World War II saw the Coast Guard participating in every amphibious operation in which the United States was involved. With each extension of his service as commandant, Waesche was promoted from rear admiral to vice-admiral to

Russell Randolph Waesche. *Courtesy of the United States Coast Guard.*

full four-star admiral, the only person to attain those consecutive ranks by the end of World War II.

Admiral Waesche greatly improved the traditional functions of the Coast Guard, always emphasizing maritime safety, icebreaking procedures and technical advances that aided navigation. He always kept those who served at the forefront of his management style, frequently making personal inspections.

When he retired on January 1, 1946, he was in ill health. He died at Bethesda Naval Hospital on October 17 that same year. He was buried at Arlington National Cemetery on October 21, with a who's who of the Coast Guard and U.S. Navy in attendance.

He was survived by his wife, the former Agnes R. Cronin, who remained in their Chevy Chase home until her death a year later. She was laid to rest beside her husband in Arlington.

Four sons also survived. They were Russell R. Jr., who would become a rear admiral in the Coast Guard; Harry Lee, a lieutenant colonel in the U.S. Army Air Force; James C., also an officer in the Coast Guard; and William, still a student in secondary school at the time of his father's death. Three sisters and three brothers also survived.

Admiral Waesche's career likely will never be duplicated. The programs he implemented before and after he became commandant of the Coast Guard, although improved since, still stand out and continue to work for the benefit of the men and women of the service and the nation.

JAMES WILKINSON

Patriot, Scoundrel and Commander of the Army

Consumed by a personality given to intrigue, James Wilkinson brought both honor and shame upon himself in a military career that spanned the Revolutionary War and the conflict of 1812. And he died an expatriate in Mexico City.

Born into a family of means in Benedict, Calvert County, Maryland, he first became a physician in the area of Frederick County south of Point of Rocks. But when the War of Independence erupted, he enlisted in George Washington's army, given the rank of captain because of his education. His service included the siege of Boston, the ill-fated foray into Canada with Benedict Arnold and the Battles of Trenton and Princeton.

From 1779 to 1783, he was the "clothier general of the army." He was mustered out when his books didn't balance, and he moved to Kentucky, laying claim to vast lands between Lexington and Louisville, playing a significant role in the opening of the Ohio and Mississippi Rivers to commerce. In that role, he developed a relationship with the Spanish government in New

General James Wilkinson. *Courtesy of the Historical Society of Frederick County.*

Orleans, which eventually led to his trial in Frederick on numerous charges, the most serious of which was treason.

He returned to the military in 1791 when President Washington offered him a commission as a colonel. He served—again with distinction—at Fallen Timbers under General "Mad" Anthony Wayne. But the officers suffered a clash of personalities and became bitter enemies. Now holding the rank of brigadier general, Wilkinson was promoted to general of the armies when Wayne died unexpectedly on December 15, 1796. He would hold that title until he left the army in 1815.

During the years following Wayne's death, Wilkinson continued to curry favor with the Spanish government in Louisiana, even signing a pledge of allegiance to Spain. When President Thomas Jefferson closed the deal for the Louisiana Purchase in 1803, Wilkinson was made governor of the territory.

Later, when former Vice President Aaron Burr was tried for treason in Richmond, the defense tried to shift the blame for Burr's action onto

Wilkinson, who was the chief prosecution witness. It apparently worked because Burr was acquitted, a decision that led eventually to the court-martial of Wilkinson in Frederick.

On September 2, 1811, Wilkinson was brought before a court-martial board at the Hessian Barracks here, charged with numerous counts revolving around his Spanish connections. Roger Brooke Taney, later Chief Justice of the United States, and John Hanson Thomas were his defense counsel. Both lawyers believed Wilkinson to be guilty of at least some of the charges but during the nearly four-month trial came to the conclusion that he was innocent. This was the second of three times Wilkinson was court-martialed. The verdict was delivered on December 25 but was not announced publicly until March 1812 because President James Madison had to approve it. Wilkinson was declared not guilty, and his rank was restored.

During the War of 1812, he commanded the unsuccessful invasion of Canada. Following that failure, he was pushed aside for younger officers and was honorably discharged in 1815.

After completing a bitter three-volume autobiography in 1816, Wilkinson returned to New Orleans, becoming a sugar planter, and again knew great success. But once more, ambition got the best of him, and in 1822, he went to Mexico City, thinking that his previous relationship with the Spanish government would enhance his chances of gaining grants to colonize parts of Texas. This dream died with him on December 25, 1825. He is buried there.

In numerous accounts of his life, James Wilkinson has been called physician, patriot, general of the army, coward, treacherous, bribe-taker, traitor, "damned old rascal," self-promoter and "the most finished scoundrel." He was likely all of these things.

OTHO HOLLAND WILLIAMS

Patriot and Progenitor of a Town

When you live in an area full of history, as we do here in Frederick, it is always refreshing to discover that a person with a direct connection to our community accomplished great deeds elsewhere.

Thus it is with Otho Holland Williams, born on March 1, 1749, in Prince George's County, Maryland. Likely before he was a year old, his parents, Joseph

Otho Holland Williams.
*Courtesy of Independence National
Historical Park.*

and Priscilla Holland Williams, moved their young family to the mouth of the Conococheague Creek in Washington County, then in Frederick County. The family lived a quiet life there until about 1761, when both Priscilla and Joseph died, leaving only a small estate to support their seven children.

Because he was the oldest, Otho, at thirteen, sought employment, which he found in the clerk's office of the Frederick County Court. He quickly mastered the job and eventually took over the clerk's job. He moved to Baltimore in 1767, becoming clerk in that court. In 1774, he returned to Frederick and went into business, all the while supporting his siblings.

When the Revolutionary War erupted in 1775, Williams immediately joined a rifle company headed by Captain Thomas Price. His reputation as a marksman impressed Price so much that he made him his lieutenant. Price's company and that of Michael Cresap—the son of perhaps the greatest pioneer in this country's history—marched to Boston in twenty-two days to join the fight, becoming the first to reinforce George Washington's men.

In an early engagement with the British, Price was wounded and Williams became captain. Just before the Declaration of Independence was written in 1776, Williams became a major in Hugh Stephenson's Maryland and Virginia Rifle Regiment and fought valiantly in a losing battle at Fort Washington, New York. Hessian soldiers captured many of the militia, including Williams, who was later imprisoned, paroled and reincarcerated due to a friendship he had developed with a British officer. For many months, he was the cellmate of the more famous Ethan Allen of the Vermont Green Mountain Boys. Williams never fully recovered from his time spent in prison; his health became permanently impaired.

After he was exchanged for the very officer whose friendship had led to his reimprisonment, he fought in the Battle of Monmouth and was later transferred to the southern command, where he became adjutant general under both Generals Horatio Gates and Nathanael Greene. In the South, Williams was a key figure in the Battle of Guilford Court House, North Carolina; Hobkirk Hill, South Carolina; and Eutaw Springs, South Carolina. He was promoted to brigadier general in 1782.

After the war, Williams, a strapping six-footer with handsome features, married Mary Smith, daughter of a wealthy Baltimore merchant, who always addressed her husband as her "dear General Williams."

During the postwar years and until his death, Williams served as a naval officer for the Port of Baltimore under both state and federal appointment.

In 1787, Williams laid out the town of Williamsport close to where he had grown up. He even met with George Washington and other government officials in 1790 when the new town was considered as the site for the nation's capital. It was quickly rejected because of a lack of navigable waters for oceangoing vessels.

As Williams's health continued to deteriorate, he took a trip to Barbados in hopes that the Caribbean climate would restore it. In the early summer of 1794, he set out for Sweet Springs at Bath, Virginia, but only got as far as Woodstock, where his condition worsened. He died on July 15 and is buried in Riverside Cemetery in Williamsport.

Despite Williams's distinguished military career, perhaps his major contribution to the history of our nation is contained in his papers now in the possession of the Maryland Historical Society. His numerous letters to both his friend Dr. Philip Thomas and to his family detail the manner in which the Revolutionary War was fought. Only a few other Patriots left such a legacy.

Ministers

WILLIAM NELSON PENDLETON
Engineer, Educator, Soldier and Minister

Fredericktonians at the start of the Civil War knew William Nelson Pendleton only as rector of All Saints Episcopal Church. However, he was far more than that. This kindly gentleman was a graduate of West Point, the first principal of Episcopal High School in Alexandria, Virginia, in 1839 and an exceptional engineer.

During the war, he rose to the rank of brigadier general in the Army of Northern Virginia, heading Robert E. Lee's artillery corps. At the Battle of Fredericksburg, he was beside Lee when Lee uttered the immortal words, "It is well war is so terrible or we should get too fond of it."

Pendleton was born into a prominent Virginia family on December 26, 1809. He entered West Point as a cadet in 1826 after his older brother declined the appointment and entered medical school. Pendleton was particularly proficient in mathematics and engineering and graduated fifth in his class. He was assigned as an artillery officer, but after a single year in the field, he returned to West Point as an instructor.

Unhappy with the direction of national politics, he resigned from the army in 1832 and took a position as a professor at a new college in Bristol, Pennsylvania. The school lasted but four years. Pendleton, however, made good use of those years, becoming an ordained Episcopal

William Nelson Pendleton. *Courtesy of All Saints Episcopal Church.*

minister. Instead of accepting a rectorship, he took a position as professor of mathematics at a Newark, Delaware college. Three years later, he was appointed the first principal of Episcopal High School, where he was able to establish the rigorous curriculum. The pay was poor, and Pendleton resigned after five years, deeply in debt. He then became rector of two parishes in Baltimore County.

On October 24, 1847, the Reverend Pendleton became rector of All Saints Parish in Frederick. However, his first job was more secular than religious. On October 7, the Carroll Creek flooded and took out the bridge on East Patrick Street. Because of his engineering background, city fathers asked him to design and oversee construction of a new bridge. He accepted, and that bridge remained in service until 1926.

Pendleton's time in Frederick was short-lived, as a dispute with the vestry over the need for a new sanctuary led to his resignation in 1853. He then became rector of Grace Parish in Lexington, Virginia.

When the Civil War erupted, being the only man in the community with artillery experience, he became the commander of the Rockbridge Artillery, which possessed four cannons. He named them Matthew, Mark, Luke and John. Shortly thereafter, he was assigned to Lee's command staff and put in charge of artillery. He and Lee, who had known each other at West Point, now became fast friends, a relationship that continued until Lee's death in 1870. During the war, Pendleton led his men in several major battles, including Falling Waters, South Mountain, Antietam and Fredericksburg.

After the war, he returned to Grace Parish and was overjoyed when Lee was appointed president of Washington College in Lexington. Lee became a vestryman at Grace Church. It was a time of great growth for the small liberal arts college, and a chapel was among the new buildings. When Lee died on October 12, 1870, Pendleton conducted his funeral in the newly completed chapel, the first service there. And as Pendleton was frequently mistaken for the great general, he was used as the model for Lee's marble sarcophagus, now in the undercroft of the chapel at what is today Washington and Lee University.

As if in a reenactment of his challenge to build a new sanctuary in Frederick, Pendleton launched a similar campaign to build a new church for Grace Parish. He traveled extensively in southwest Virginia, gathering funds for the project.

Once again, fate intervened in Pendleton's life. His funeral, following his death on January 15, 1883, was the first service held in the new sanctuary of Grace Episcopal Church.

ROBERT RICHFORD ROBERTS

Backwoods Bishop

Life in America was arduous, to say the least, as our nation developed. Families were separated by miles of bad "country" roads; horses and wagons were the only means of transportation. So it was into this world that Robert Richford Roberts was born on August 2, 1778, on a small Frederick County farm, God's Gift, named by his parents. His father, Robert Morgan Roberts, fought in the Revolution and spent that long winter of 1777 at Valley Forge.

Young Robert was the seventh of eleven children and had little formal education. His mother, Mary Richford Roberts, taught him to read at age four, and he developed into an avid reader, although the only book available was the Bible. For the most part he was self-educated, attending school only sporadically.

Bishop Robert R. Roberts.
*Courtesy of DePauw University,
Greencastle, Indiana.*

When he was seven, the family moved to the Ligonier Valley in western Pennsylvania, east of Pittsburgh. Here, although further separated from established society, the family flourished. Raised as Episcopalians in Frederick at All Saints Church, they converted to Methodism in Pennsylvania because that was the only church in their community. Gifted with a strong voice, the tall and handsome Roberts soon became a spiritual leader, as ministers were few and far between.

He married Elizabeth "Betsey" Oldham in 1799. She was a daughter of longtime family friends, going back to Maryland's Eastern Shore before the Robertses moved to Frederick County. Although they raised several children of family members, they had none of their own.

As the years passed into the nineteenth century, the call to the ministry intensified. Roberts resisted as long as he could, insisting that he had other work to do. As he worked to clear his farmland, he would often rest on a stump and "preach to the trees." His voice was "deep and musical," and he had an "accurate ear for sounds." With encouragement from Betsey, he completed the requirement to become a circuit rider and was ordained by Bishop Francis Asbury in 1802.

Being a Methodist minister in those days was a tough assignment, as churches were separated by many miles and services were usually held in houses rather than in sanctuaries. He did get home to see "his Betsey" when his travels took him nearby. During his years as a circuit rider, Bishop Asbury assigned him to the East Coast for eight years, where he served—with great distinction—churches in Baltimore, Northern Virginia and his hometown of Frederick, where he renewed childhood friendships.

After his elevation to bishop in 1816, he was assigned to the frontier, becoming the first prelate west of the Alleghenies. He and Betsey moved to Lawrenceport, Indiana. His work now became more difficult, as he traveled as many as five thousand miles each year on horseback, serving churches as far away as Mississippi, Louisiana, western Tennessee and Arkansas. Other southern states were also the beneficiary of his ministry. The annual conferences of the Methodists were held in the East, so Bishop Roberts traveled yearly more than one thousand miles to attend.

His annual salary was $200. There are records that indicate that he donated half of it to Indiana Asbury University in Greencastle, now known as DePauw University.

The constant traveling in all sorts of weather took its toll on the bishop. It became more and more difficult as the years passed. Although he was home in late December 1842, he still made day trips to area churches "to serve God and his children." In early January 1843, he preached his last sermon.

During the next several months, his health deteriorated, and he died on Sunday morning, March 26, at his Lawrenceport home. His funeral was held the following Tuesday, but his burial was delayed by a violent storm, reminiscent of the many he endured as a preacher and bishop.

In January 1844, his remains were taken to the university campus in Greencastle and reinterred. When Betsey died on December 17, 1858, she was buried beside him.

Physicians

Victor Francis Cullen
Dedicated to a Cure

His name is familiar to most who have been in Frederick County for even a short time. But few know very much about Victor Francis Cullen, who was the superintendent of the Maryland Tuberculosis Sanatorium at Sabillasville in northwest Frederick County from 1909 until his forced retirement on January 1, 1946.

Dr. Cullen's story is one of dedication to a single disease, which attacked him while he was completing his residency at Baltimore's St. Joseph's Hospital. He became a patient at a Blue Ridge Summit (Pennsylvania) facility dedicated to the care of TB patients. The only treatment in those days was rest and fresh air, and because his case was mild, he recovered quickly.

In 1906, Maryland's Tuberculosis Commission selected Loop Mountain at Sabillasville as the site for the state's first facility for TB patients because of its 1,500-foot elevation and magnificent views in all directions. Construction began shortly afterward but was exceedingly slow. Dr. Cullen, while recovering, offered his services free of charge to the patients at Sabillasville, who lived in rustic conditions. On January 1, 1909, he was appointed superintendent. It was quickly evident to state officials that Dr. Cullen was the expert they needed to lead the battle against TB across Maryland.

Victor Francis Cullen (front row, center) with his staff. *Courtesy of the Historical Society of Frederick County.*

During his early years in charge, Dr. Cullen not only oversaw the many construction projects there but also designed many of the buildings. He even established a school on site to train nurses specifically in the treatment of TB patients. These women were much sought after by TB hospitals across the country.

His most lasting legacy in the Sabillasville community was perhaps the farm he established, employing many local men and women to work it. The farm and adjacent orchard provided much of the food the patients consumed, saving countless state taxpayer funds.

Dr. Cullen also ran a company store, was a notary public, was postmaster for the sanatorium, was instrumental in getting a railroad to the site and was the first doctor to examine each patient seeking admittance. Before his forced retirement—because he had reached the mandatory retirement age of sixty-five—he oversaw the establishment of three other facilities in Maryland for the treatment of tuberculosis: at Henryton in Carroll County, at Mount Wilson in Baltimore and at Salisbury.

Born in Funkstown in Washington County on September 5, 1881, he was the son of Martin E. and Margaret Cushwa Cullen. He attended local schools before he matriculated at Rock Hill College in Ellicott City. Upon graduation, he was admitted to Johns Hopkins School of Medicine. He planned to be a surgeon and was working toward that goal when he was stricken with TB. Seldom has an illness led to a career as successful as Dr. Cullen's.

He was so devoted to his work that he put his personal life on hold while he developed positive treatments far beyond those known at the time. He even became the first doctor in Maryland to employ X-ray in the diagnosis of TB. He was married in 1926 at the age of forty-five to Ethel Clare Bell, the daughter of a prominent Lutheran minister of the day. They had one child: a daughter, Jeanne Margaret.

At a retirement dinner at the Emerson Hotel in Baltimore, speaker after speaker lauded Dr. Cullen and his accomplishments. Judge Samuel K. Dennis summed it up by saying, "I know of no man who has done more for others than Dr. Cullen."

It was then that the hospital at Sabillasville was named the Victor F. Cullen Sanatorium. Today, with advances in the treatment of TB, the Sabillasville facility is used as a treatment center for at-risk juveniles.

Dr. Cullen suffered a stroke on the morning of March 9, 1949, and was taken to Baltimore's Union Memorial Hospital, where he died that afternoon. Services were held at SS Phillip and James Roman Catholic Church in Baltimore. He was buried at Rose Hill Cemetery in Hagerstown.

BERNARD OSCAR THOMAS SR.

Dedicated to a Community's Health

Advertisements for Lifebuoy Health Soap were the first things that came to mind as I entered the offices of Dr. Bernard Oscar Thomas Sr. in 1952 as a twelve-year-old new resident of Frederick. But they were not the lasting memory of the man some said brought half the residents of Frederick County into the world during his fifty-nine-year medical career.

From humble beginnings on a farm near Adamstown, Maryland, on November 6, 1882, to the pinnacle of love and respect in the county he called home for all but two of his eighty-six years, Dr. B.O., as he was known, left a lasting impression. He was a grandfatherly type in my youth, using skills and common-sense solutions to medical problems, mixing in an engaging personality.

After his early education in public schools, he entered the University of Maryland School of Medicine in Baltimore and, immediately upon graduation, opened an office in New Market. Two years later, he moved his practice to Frederick, where he remained until he retired in 1965.

For most of his working life, he had offices in the Professional Building on North Market Street, although his hours there were limited by his

attention to patients at Frederick City (Memorial) Hospital, the Montevue Home and Emergency Hospital and to those too ill to come to him.

Recently, an elderly woman sitting in a doctor's office related how Dr. B.O. often came to her parents' farmhouse to care for a family member in the middle of the night. "He loved to sit around and talk after tending to the sick person," she said, "often staying through breakfast."

Dr. Bernard O. Thomas. *From Tercentenary History of Maryland.*

Dr. Bernard O. Thomas. *Courtesy of the Thomas family.*

When World War I erupted in 1917, he enlisted as a lieutenant in the U.S. Army Medical Corps, rising to the rank of captain before being discharged in May 1919. He came back to Frederick, remaining a respected physician for another forty-six years.

In the early years of the Depression, it became painfully obvious to all that the Montevue Home on Rosemont Avenue was inadequate to accommodate the mentally ill and the poor, particularly its limited medical facilities. So a plan was devised to convert the old Tramp House at the rear of the home into a hospital. On June 9, 1934, Emergency Hospital opened. Dr. B.O. was among the first physicians to offer his services. The story goes that he delivered the first baby there—and the last in 1955 when the facility closed. He often spoke of the great joy he received from his work there, giving so much of himself to help the less fortunate.

As his career dwindled down, he took on the demanding job of county medical examiner, still willing to be called out in the middle of the night to lend his expertise whenever it was needed.

His personal life took on added pleasure in 1909 when he married Margaret Lee Barthlow. They became the parents of two sons, both of whom followed in their father's footsteps, practicing medicine beside him in the Professional Building.

Throughout his career, Dr. B.O. lent his congenial personality to other civic endeavors as well. He was a charter member of the Kiwanis Club of Frederick and an active and devoted member of All Saints Episcopal Church. He served as a trustee for both the Maryland School for the Deaf and Hood College, and he was very active in various Masonic orders.

When he decided to retire, his friends threw a Stag Party, during which he was presented a plaque naming him "Frederick's #1 Citizen." It was also during that year of 1965 that Dr. B.O. became the first Frederick County citizen to sign up for Medicare.

In the early morning hours of April 15, 1969, he passed away at his Watkins Acres home at eighty-six. Largely attended final rites were held at All Saints, with burial following in Mount Olivet Cemetery.

This kindly gentleman is still remembered today as just an old country doctor, one who loved what he did and those to whom he was able to provide some small measure of a better life.

JOHN TYLER
Pioneering Oculist

As time marches on, the details of the lives and accomplishments of our forebears get stretched to the less-than-believable stage. Such is the case with Dr. John Tyler.

It has been recounted countless times that he performed the first cataract operation in the United States. And while it is true that he did perform that surgery, it is likely that he was just the first to do so in this region. Actually, what he performed was called "couching," whereby he would push the cataract aside, never totally removing it, as is done today.

Tyler was born on June 29, 1763, in Prince George's County. Little is known of his early life, including the names of his parents. However, it is likely that he attended local schools, possibly not even public at that time. Without confirming facts, Philadelphia is perhaps where he received his

Dr. John Tyler. *Courtesy of Artist YEMI, from* Pillars of Frederick.

medical education, such as it was in those days, because that city was the hub of advanced medical education in the late eighteenth century.

On January 17, 1786, he opened his medical practice in Frederick, becoming one of many doctors in town at the time. That could explain his specialization in diseases of the eye. The location of his first office is lost to history, but in the 1790s, he built the house at what is today 108 West Church Street. The house contained nine rooms, providing ample space for his office and residence.

Tyler was an active participant in the affairs of the community. In 1800, he was an elector for Thomas Jefferson, then just the president-in-waiting. After that highly visible participation, he seems to have disappeared from local notice, as the surviving newspapers of the day carry no mention of him other than to name him as a plaintiff or defendant in various lawsuits, all of which concerned local—rather than personal—issues.

He did resurface, as history tells us, in 1814, when he got wind that city officials were planning to extend Record Street, along which stood the old Frederick Academy, through to Patrick Street. In his efforts to stop this project, he became aware of a local ordinance that said that if a substantial building was under construction in the path of the street extension, the city could not halt its completion. Within just days, Tyler began building the foundation for what is known today as the Spite House. Tyler's concern arose from his belief that large wagons with heavy loads would rumble down the new part of Record Street next to his "operating" room, thus jeopardizing his delicate work.

In front of his home today is an iron dog, which got its name from a later owner of the property, Edward Eichelberger, an attorney. It seems that when children would hop on the dog's back, Eichelberger would open the door to greet them. When asked the dog's name, he would always reply, "Guess!" Of course, the children would call out all sorts of names, none of which was the correct answer. Thus, the name "Guess" remains with us today.

Another story concerning the dog is that Confederate soldiers removed it and hauled it away to make bullets for their weapons. The story went that Union forces chased the Rebels out of town, forcing them to abandon their "prize" in Carroll Creek, to be returned to its post guarding the steps of the Eichelberger residence by Union soldiers. Researchers for years have attempted to verify this story, but to no avail.

On September 7, 1831, Catherin Contee Tyler, the doctor's wife, died at age sixty-one. She was buried in All Saints Cemetery on East All Saints Street. However, obituaries made no mention of survivors other than her husband.

And when Tyler died on October 15, 1841, he, too, was laid to rest in that church's cemetery. Once again, available death notices, including Jacob Engelbrecht's diary, failed to mention any survivors other than his brother, Dr. William Tyler. In December 1913, the remains of Tyler and his wife were exhumed and reinterred at Mount Olivet Cemetery.

Reprinted with permission from Pillars of Frederick, *2011, Great State Publishing LLC*

Philanthropists

JOHN LOATS
Answering His Community's Needs

Frederick has produced numerous philanthropists throughout its history. Names such as Rosenstock, Weinberg and Delaplaine come quickly to mind. But one name likely escapes notoriety even though every college-bound student should pay close attention to it: John Loats.

He was born in Baltimore County on October 7, 1814, the son of Henry and Elizabeth Loats, both immigrants from Germany. Less than three years later, Henry Loats died, leaving a widow without any real means of support. Before John reached the age of eleven, he was working full time, providing for his mother, as had his older sibling during those intervening years.

He acquired only eight months of formal education and was apprenticed to George Algire, a local tanner. John was diligent in applying himself and quickly learned all aspects of that business. In 1835, he formed a partnership with Richard Johns in the tanning business, an association that lasted thirteen years. Loats sold his interest and moved to Frederick in 1848.

Loats purchased the tannery of Casper Quinn, including a large home. Later that year, a flood of the Carroll Creek wiped him out, as it did several other tanneries along the banks of the creek. He rebuilt and became one of the largest and most respected tanners in Maryland, producing some of the finest leather products in the age of saddles and buggies.

The Loats Orphanage. *Courtesy of the Historical Society of Frederick County.*

He also acquired a profitable farm at the south end of Frederick and used it to some extent to provide produce for the less fortunate in the community. Perhaps this was the start of his willingness to give back to his fellow citizens.

Loats also gave of his time to other local pursuits. He was the president of the Frederick and Pennsylvania Railroad, overseeing the construction of the road; and he was active in local agricultural societies, holding several offices. He was also a Frederick City alderman for a time.

But it was his membership in the Evangelical Lutheran Church that led to his enduring legacy. He was present in 1867 when the church's pastor, Dr. George Diehl, issued a challenge to the congregation to establish an orphanage. In 1871, Loats purchased—for $14,000—the former home of Dr. John Baltzell, across the street from his church, setting in motion an answer to Dr. Diehl's pleas.

Upon his death on March 24, 1879, Loats left his property—both his farm and his home on East Church Street next door to Winchester Hall—to the church for the purpose of establishing a home for orphaned girls. There was one stipulation, however, which delayed the project. Loats left the property to his sister-in-law, Anna Josephine Sifford, until her death or marriage. Ms. Sifford married in July 1881, and the Loats Female Orphan Asylum became a reality. For the next seventy-seven years, between six and fifteen girls at any one time made their home at 24 East Church Street. Profits from the farm were also used to fund the facility.

With the advent of government-funded social programs, the necessity for the orphanage dwindled. In 1958, the Loats Asylum was closed and the property sold to the Historical Society of Frederick County, which continues to operate it as a museum and research facility.

With the proceeds from the sale of the Loats home and, over the years, the sale of parts of the farm, Evangelical Lutheran Church, through the Loats Foundation, Inc., now provides scholarships for Frederick County students attending any Maryland college or university or Shepherd University in nearby West Virginia. Applications are available in the financial aid offices of those institutions.

Although he had no children of his own, John Loats has provided countless Frederick County children with opportunities they otherwise would not have had, a legacy that continues to live.

SAMUEL H. ROSENSTOCK

"Mr. Sam" and "Hon"

Rosenstock! Now there is a name to reckon with in Frederick. For most of the twentieth century, Samuel Heidelberger Rosenstock was a giant in the business community, but he is likely most remembered today for the financial support he and his wife provided to many local organizations, including Hood College, Frederick Memorial Hospital and the Salvation Army.

Perhaps unknown to almost everyone who knew him, "Mr. Sam," as he was affectionately known, was eccentric. He kept these quirks mostly to himself, though they began when he was a child and convinced his mother, after his father's early death, to move to Frederick.

Throughout most of his adult life, he insisted on having a glass of freshly squeezed orange juice for breakfast. And if he didn't get it, it was "hell to pay" for the person preparing his meal. He even got to the point of changing his will because he was given a glass of frozen juice.

For some reason, and at a point early in his life, he began collecting liquor miniatures—not those that come in nondescript bottles but the ones in every shape imaginable, like animals and flowers. When he died in 1981,

Mr. Sam (far left) and Hon (second from left) with Frances W. Ashbury and the Reverend Maurice D. Ashbury. *From the author's collection.*

at age ninety-five, he had more than five thousand stored on shelves he had specially built for their display.

When Dr. Dana Cable was dating Mr. Sam's niece, they became good friends. During a conversation in his study, Dr. Cable asked Mr. Sam what he was going to do with the miniatures. He was politely told that they were to be sold as part of his estate. Dr. Cable asked, as he headed for the door, if Mr. Sam would consider leaving them to him. The next day, Mr. Sam changed his will, leaving the miniatures and the shelving to Dr. Cable. Since then, the collection has continued to grow.

Mr. Sam was an astute businessman, becoming manager of the Frederick City Packing Company at nineteen and acquiring a one-third interest in the plant at twenty-one.

During World War I, he served on the U.S. Food Administration. When a colleague there mentioned morale was low among soldiers in Europe because they were unable to obtain whiskey, he told the administrator that he could solve the problem. One of the products the packing company was producing for the war effort was canned tomato juice. So, in short order, specially marked cans of "tomato juice" were headed to France. Morale increased quickly upon the arrival of the "juice."

In 1946, he sold his packing plants in Frederick and Thurmont to Jenkins Brothers and began a thirty-five-year career of providing financial support to the community. Hood College named a building for "Mr. Sam" and "Hon," as he called his wife, the former Henrietta Kaufman. They met when he was a runner for a Wall Street firm and she was among the first women to ever work in that financial district. "Hon" also served her country during World War I as one of only eight female chief petty officers in the navy.

"Mr. Sam" and "Hon" never forgot their humble beginning and even saw to it that several young people were able to attend college.

A particular concern through their lives was the spiritual upbringing of the children of the community. A classic example of their concern began in 1950 when Dr. William Schnauffer III died unexpectedly. The surgeon had a young son, just four years old at the time. For years, "Mr. Sam" took the youngster to All Saints Episcopal Church whenever he was asked, and that was frequently. William Schnauffer IV, now the owner of a hearing testing firm in Illinois, has never forgotten the special kindness shown to him by this man of the Jewish faith.

Sam and Henrietta Rosenstock have passed into the annals of Frederick history, but their legacy and thoughtfulness will remain for generations to come. Children, grandchildren and great-grandchildren of those who benefited from their generosity will forever remember "Mr. Sam" and "Hon" for the people they were as well as what they did.

Politicians

DANIEL DULANY THE YOUNGER
Faithful to the Crown to the End

The phrase "like father like son" certainly applies in the Dulany family of Maryland. Daniel, the father, was a force in the state in its infancy, even laying out Fredericktown in 1745. The son Daniel was perhaps even more influential as the colonies fought for independence in the waning years of the eighteenth century.

While his father turned his attention to the development of vast areas of western Maryland, Daniel Dulany the Younger, as he was known even after his father's death in 1753, developed a reputation as the final arbiter in many ticklish legal matters facing the government in the days of the proprietorship of the Lords Baltimore.

Born in Annapolis on June 28, 1722, the eldest son of Daniel and Rebecca Smith, Dulany received his preliminary education mostly through tutors before being sent to England, where he attended Eton College and Clare Hall of Cambridge University. After his legal education at Middle Temple at the Inns of Court in London, he was called to the bar in 1746, a rare accomplishment for a "colonist" in the days before the Revolutionary War.

It wasn't long afterward that Young Daniel returned to Maryland and immediately set foot into court proceedings around the state, being admitted to the practice of law in 1747 in the Court of Chancery and Prince George's

Daniel Dulany the Younger.
From Pillars of Maryland.

and Anne Arundel Counties. In the late winter of 1749, he was admitted to the Frederick County bar.

His political career began that year when he was elected to the Lower House of the Maryland legislature from Fredericktown, but the entire election was voided later that year. It was also in that year (September 16) that he married Rebecca Tasker, the daughter of Benjamin Tasker, who owned vast areas in Frederick County, including the area on which Daniel Dulany the Elder laid out Fredericktown.

During the next thirty years, his involvement in state and local politics grew along with his influence. His opinions, however, moved from support of the colonies' thirst for freedom to a staunch neutrality advocacy as the push for independence progressed, the result of which was the confiscation of all his property by the state in 1781 because he was a Tory.

Following the passage of the Stamp Act in March 1765, Dulany published a denunciation of its imposition on those who had no representation in the British Parliament. It received such wide recognition that William Pitt based his highly praised speech to Parliament in defiance of the law on the premises contained in Dulany's pamphlet.

But as the years passed, Dulany became increasingly an opponent of armed conflict to obtain separation from England. In 1773, he and Charles Carroll of Carrollton carried on a lengthy discussion of the issues involved in a series of newspaper articles, with the obvious result that he was on the losing side in the debate as far as the general public was concerned.

After his father's death on December 5, 1753, Young Dulany continued to purchase real estate of Frederick County in addition to the lots in Fredericktown he inherited from his father. On November 9, 1767, he acquired eight thousand acres previously owned by Lord Baltimore as part of the proprietor's Conococheague Manor. An area of this purchase was known as Red Hill, what we know today as Prospect Hall. It was on this property that Dulany the Younger supposedly built the mansion that served as a Catholic educational facility for the past forty years.

After his property was taken, Dulany retired to private life and concerned himself infrequently with public affairs. But his reputation as a lawyer remained intact until his death on March 17, 1797. He was buried at Old St. Paul's Church in Baltimore.

One historian wrote, "He was regarded as an oracle of the law. It was the constant practice of the Court of the Province to submit to his opinion every question of difficulty which came before them and so infallible were his opinions considered, that he who hoped to reverse them was regarded as 'hoping against hope.'"

ENOCH LOUIS LOWE

Enigmatic Politician and Governor

Frederick is justly proud of the fact that its citizens have the understanding and foresight to overlook a candidate's age when selecting its leaders. Mayor Ron Young, at twenty-nine, and his son, Blaine, an alderman at twenty-five, served the city of Frederick with distinction. But they play second fiddle when compared to Enoch Louis Lowe, the youngest man ever elected governor of the Free State.

There is some dispute as to just where Lowe was born, but it is well established that it was somewhere in Frederick County. Some sources say Frederick City; others cite his maternal grandmother's estate, the Hermitage, along the Monocacy River east of town. He was born on

August 10, 1820, and it is certain that he spent his early years with his grandmother, as his parents, Bradley S.A. and Adelaide Vincendiere Lowe, were divorced.

His early education was at St. John's School. His mother's family felt a stronger education was needed for him, so they sent Lowe to Clongowas Wood College near Dublin, Ireland. After three years there, he transferred to the Jesuit College at Stonyhurst at Lancashire. Upon graduation in 1839, he made a grand tour of Europe.

Young Lowe then entered the study of law and, in 1842, was admitted to the bar. He formed a partnership with John W. Baughman, who would soon become owner and editor of

Enoch Louis Lowe. *Courtesy of the Historical Society of Frederick County.*

the *Examiner.* He also stuck his foot into political waters. In 1845, he was elected to the House of Delegates, where he championed a complete rewrite of the state's constitution. His eloquence and determination gained him a growing leadership role in the General Assembly.

Although he was not constitutionally eligible due to his age, he was nominated to be governor by the Democrats in 1850; he defeated his opponent, Whig William B. Clarke, of Washington County, by nearly 1,500 votes, the majority of which came from Baltimore City. Discerning voters there were apparently the rule of the day, as Baltimore elected a Whip mayor in the same election. Governor Lowe attained the proper age before the election and was sworn into office in January 1851. His administration was remarkable, as the state's constitution was rewritten and stands today; the B&O Railroad was completed to the Ohio River; prison terms for debt were abolished; and, perhaps most significant to Maryland citizens, state taxes were reduced by 40 percent and the state deficit was eliminated.

After his term as governor ended in 1854, Lowe rose in the ranks of his party and was influential at the Democratic Party Convention in 1856, which nominated James Buchanan of Pennsylvania. The president offered Lowe the position of ambassador to China, but he declined and returned to his law practice.

The rumblings of war were becoming louder with each passing year, and Lowe supported the Southern cause, convinced that Maryland would secede. With the outbreak of hostilities, he went to Richmond, where he was greeted with great respect and fanfare by the Virginia assembly. His reputation as an eloquent speaker had preceded him.

During the war, he moved frequently, mostly throughout Georgia. In November 1865, he returned to Frederick but stayed only a few months before moving to Brooklyn, New York, where he felt he would be better able to support his wife and eleven children. Although often sought out by New York politicians to become involved, Governor Lowe seemed to care only for the peace and quiet of his family and home and thus occupied himself out of the sight and bustle of a busy world.

He died on August 23, 1892, following an unsuccessful operation for gout. His body was returned to Frederick, where services were conducted at St. John the Evangelist Roman Catholic Church, just a block from his former home at the corner of East Second and present-day Maxwell Avenue. He was buried in the church's cemetery.

Successful Families

ROGER NELSON AND JOHN NELSON
Like Father, Like Son—Sort Of

Men in the early history of Frederick County offered their services in various and sundry ways. Taney, Key, Johnson, Hanson, Everhart are names that slip from the tongue easily. Perhaps Nelson should be added to the list, as a father and son appear prominently from the time of the American Revolution to the beginning of the Civil War.

Roger Nelson was born in June 1759 at Hopeland in southern Frederick County, on Dr. Arthur Nelson's Point of Rocks Plantation. At the beginning of the Revolution, young Roger was a student at William and Mary College. When he turned twenty, he enlisted in a cavalry troop commanded by Colonel William Washington and rode south to defend the Carolinas, then controlled by the British. At the disastrous engagement at Camden, South Carolina, he lay severely wounded on the battlefield. A British officer, in passing by, struck Nelson's hand with the flat of his sword, breaking the bones of his fingers. Had he yelled for "quarter," it is likely he would have been killed, but he was unconscious. He was later revived and taken to Charleston as a prisoner.

In December 1780, Nelson was among the prisoners exchanged and rejoined Washington cavalry in time to participate in the American victory at Cowpens. He was also involved in the Battle of Guilford Courthouse, where

Attorney General John Nelson. *Courtesy of the U.S. Department of Justice.*

he was again wounded, and at Eutaw Springs. And he was at Yorktown when General Charles Lord Cornwallis surrendered to George Washington.

After the war, Roger Nelson continued his military career, rising to the rank of brigadier general in the Maryland Militia. He even commanded a cavalry troop in the suppression of the Whiskey Rebellion in 1794.

During these years, he practiced law in Frederick and quickly gained prominence. He was elected to the Maryland General Assembly in 1795 and again in 1801. He was elected to Congress in 1804 and served until he resigned in 1810 to become a judge of the Sixth Judicial Circuit Court. He continued in that position until his death on June 7, 1815. He is buried in Mount Olivet Cemetery.

John Nelson was the fourth child of Roger and Mary Brooke Sim Nelson and was born on June 1, 1791, in Frederick. He graduated from William and

Mary in 1811 and immediately began the study of the law. He was admitted to the bar in 1813. His polished manner and quick legal mind gained him a large practice.

He served a single term in Congress, from 1821 to 1823, during which time he renewed his friendship with future President John Tyler, a classmate at William and Mary.

In 1831, President Andrew Jackson asked Nelson to become his chargé d'affaire to the Two Sicilies to settle a dispute with the monarch there. He accepted, and when he returned to the United States in 1832 from a successful mission, he moved his law practice to Baltimore.

In 1843, President Tyler, who had succeeded William Henry Harrison, asked Nelson to become his attorney general, a position to which he was quickly confirmed. During these years as attorney general, he also served for a short time as acting secretary of state, holding both positions at the same time.

When he retired as attorney general in March 1845, John Nelson returned to his private practice in Baltimore, where he was revered by his colleagues. Upon his death on January 8, 1860, Reverdy Johnson, himself a respected and admired barrister, said of him, "I have heard more eloquence, more brilliant imagery, more power of amplification, and more affluence of learning, but I do not think that in force of analysis, clearness of arrangement, perspicuity of statement, simplicity of language, closeness of logic, and concentration of thought I have even seen him much, if at all, excelled."

John Nelson was twice married and fathered seven children, all of whom are mentioned by name in his will. He is buried at Greenmount Cemetery in Baltimore.

The William Schnauffers

Memories May Fade, but This Family's Legacy Remains Intact

The Schnauffer name has vanished from Frederick County, but the legacy of those who bore the name will live for generations to come. In banking and medical circles, Schnauffer men made a lasting impression on the history of our community.

William Schnauffer, the banker and B&O Railroad man and the first of his family in Frederick County, was the second of five men to bear that name. He was the son of William and Elise Moos Schnauffer, who came

to America in the early 1850s. William's brother and Elise's first husband, Carl Heinrich Schnauffer, had fled Germany in 1848 after a failed revolution. When Carl arrived in Baltimore, he established a daily German-language newspaper called the *Wecker*. After his untimely death of typhoid fever in 1854, his widow continued as editor.

Elise was the daughter of wealthy Baden merchants and had an excellent education at a time when women weren't expected to seek formal training in the arts. She and her brother-in-law were married in 1859 and had three children, William II, Lillie and Emma. Together they operated the newspaper until it ceased publication in 1889. However, from about 1873 until his death, William was more interested in financial and banking matters, which sparked an interest in his son.

Top: William Schnauffer I. *Courtesy of the Schnauffer family.*

Bottom: William Schnauffer II. *Courtesy of the Schnauffer family.*

Opposite: William Schnauffer III. *Courtesy of the Schnauffer family.*

William Schnauffer II was born on June 23, 1866, and graduated from Baltimore's City College. After working at the *Wecker*, he took business courses and joined his father in financial pursuits. Two years after his father died in 1889, William the Second moved to Brunswick and within a few years started the Savings Bank of Brunswick on Potomac Street, where Brunswick Town Hall is located today.

He had other interests as well, including the Brunswick and Middletown Electric Railroad Company and the Harpers Ferry, West Virginia Light and Power Company. He was involved in the retail furniture business, a construction company and the Lovettsville and Berlin Bridge Company. Remarkably, he took just one day's vacation each year to attend the Army-Navy football game. He sold his interest in the Savings Bank to the Bank of Brunswick around 1915 and went to work for the railroad.

William Schnauffer II was married on December 15, 1897, to Mary West. The couple had four children, one of whom was born on April 8, 1903, and was named William. The third man to bear the name attended Brunswick schools and graduated from the George Washington University. He received his medical degree from the Medical College of Virginia in 1933.

He returned to Brunswick, opened a practice and the next year established the Schnauffer Hospital on A Street in an apartment over his brother West's automobile garage. Four years later, he built a larger facility for the hospital on West B Street. His renown as a surgeon spread throughout Frederick County, and he moved his practice to the county seat in 1946. He and his wife, the former Katherine Remsburg of Lewistown, had purchased the Spite House on West Church Street in 1942. They had two children: Katherine, now Mrs. Paul Sarver of Allentown, Pennsylvania, and William IV.

Dr. Schnauffer was stricken by creeping paralysis on April 7, 1950, and died the next day, leaving a void in the local medical community.

Early in his schooling, it was uncovered that William IV (known to all as Billy) was severely dyslexic. His mother was introduced to Margaret Rawson, a Frederick resident who was an outspoken advocate for children with this disorder, and she became Billy's tutor for several years. William Schnauffer IV is the CEO of the TK Group, Inc., a hearing testing company headquartered in Rockford, Illinois.

Billy married Judy Hardwick of Cleveland, Tennessee, in 1969, and they are the parents of two children: Katherine, a currency commodities trader in Chicago; and a son William V, a commercial pilot, who also flies fighter jets for the Air National Guard.

The Schnauffer legacy remains intact, and as memories fade, the family advocacy for Brunswick will live on, as will their adherence to the needs of the entire Frederick County community.

Public Servants

WILLIAM TYLER PAGE
Public Servant, Historian and Patriot

Schoolchildren of a few generations ago knew his name and memorized his one-hundred-word creed of American patriotism. But today, only a few, even in Frederick, cherish this great public servant, historian and patriot.

William Tyler Page grew up on Record Street behind the Frederick County Courthouse, now Frederick City Hall. His father was disabled when he was just ten years old, so he found employment as a printer's devil in a local paper bag factory. He didn't stay there long. His mother, Nannie Tyler Page, called upon a friend whose marriage proposal she had rejected in favor of Walker Yates Page to find her son a position in Washington, D.C. On December 19, 1881, William Tyler Page, arriving on a milk train, began his first day as a congressional page, launching a career in the House of Representatives that would last almost sixty-one years. That first day, young Page got into a fight with another youngster who made fun of the suit he was wearing, which had been sewn just the night before by his mother who stayed up all night to provide her son with suitable attire.

During his tenure in the House, Page witnessed the inauguration of fifteen presidents and watched as the United States grew from thirty-five to forty-eight states. He was voted clerk of the House in 1919 and served in that capacity until 1931. Such was the esteem in which he was held by the

William Tyler
Page. *Courtesy of
the Historical Society
of Frederick County.*

congressmen that the now majority Democrats named him minority clerk, a
position created just for him.

But it is for his authorship of the American's Creed for which Page is
best remembered. When a childhood friend, Winfield Scott Schley, led the
successful sea Battle of Santiago, Cuba, on July 3, 1898, Page was struck with
a patriotic fervor that remained until his death on October 20, 1942. Page
then began his practice of retiring to his study every July 4 to examine the
great documents of American history—the Declaration of Independence, the
Constitution, the Federalist Papers and biographies of our founding fathers.

On a clear Sunday in early 1917, returning from church where he recited
the Apostles' Creed, Page was inspired to enter a contest sponsored by the
City of Baltimore seeking a statement of American national patriotism. He
felt it should be shorter than the 109 words of the Christian creed, which

is based on the Bible. So he set about his task using the basic doctrines and tenets of Americanism. There were more than three thousand entries, and the judges, who ranked among the great names in American literature at the time, selected Page's submission. On April 3, 1918, at the height of World War I, Page received his $1,000 prize. Three days later, he purchased a Liberty Bond from Hollywood stars, including Mary Pickford and Douglas Fairbanks, on the steps of the Capitol, again reiterating his passion for America.

Upon his death the day after his seventy-fourth birthday, the *Washington Post* wrote, "No man in our times had a more profound or encyclopedic knowledge of Congress than William Tyler Page." Congressman Charles Eaton of New Jersey said from the floor of the House that he "was a courtly Christian gentleman of the old school. He belonged to the golden age when men in this country had ideals when there was an occasional sweeping of the wide white skylines of the Kingdom of God in men's thinking, and when they realized that America was not simply land, money and material things, but America was a beautiful soul, and an American was a man whose soul responded to the soul of America." Another congressman added, "Advancing steadily through diligent application, faithful service, and abiding loyalty, [Page] served through the terms of fourteen speakers and through the terms of eleven presidents—a record of service and achievements without a parallel in the history of our beloved nation."

But the authorship of the American's Creed will always remain his legacy.

Just Plain Folks

Mother Ambrosia
Elizabeth "Rose" Clarke
A Life of Dedication

She gave birth to twenty-four children, but it was her resolute dedication to veterans of our nation's armed forces that earned her the name "Mother."

Ambrosia, "Rose" to her contemporaries, was born into humble surroundings in Baltimore on August 4, 1895, to Michael and Elizabeth Derwart. Her father operated a saloon and a small convenience store next door in Locust Point. It may be that her devotion to veterans was incubated in her early years, as her father's businesses catered to sailors birthed in Baltimore's harbor.

When just twenty years old, she married Charles H. "Jerry" Clarke, a route salesman for a bakery. Part of his weekly trips took him to northern Frederick County, and it wasn't long before the couple moved to Thurmont. A few years later, Jerry quit his job and the couple opened a small restaurant. However, with so many children—even though eleven died at birth—Mrs. Clarke stayed home to corral the rest and provide a warm and hospitable place for them. She rose at 4:30 a.m. to pack their lunches and prepare an assembly-line breakfast. As would be expected, all the children had chores on the small farmette that provided much of the food they consumed.

Ambrosia E. "Mother" Clarke. *Courtesy of the Maryland Room, C. Burr Artz Library/*Frederick News-Post.

At the start of World War II, she was among the first Marylanders to donate blood, traveling to Baltimore's Fort Howard hospital to do so. It was on that first trip that her desire to help veterans began in earnest. Before she was forced to stop her blood donations by her doctors, she donated nearly sixty pints—always at military hospitals.

And so it was that "Mother" Clarke devoted the rest of her life to the task of bringing smiles to the young men she called "her boys." Thousands upon thousands of veterans cheered up when she appeared in the wards of Bethesda Naval Hospital, Walter Reed Army Hospital and the hospitals at Fort Meade and Fort Howard. The VA hospital at Martinsburg, West Virginia, was added to her list during the Korean conflict.

She made a special effort for Christmas and Easter, gathering small gifts for "her boys." She solicited them from every store she could visit in Thurmont, Frederick, Baltimore and even New York. Her visits away from home garnered unexpected hospitality from local hotels that provided her with room and board while she was in town. One year, she wrapped nearly seven hundred individual presents.

Her work for the veterans was widely recognized. She even appeared on the radio program *Queen for a Day* on December 5, 1947. But every gift she received was converted to something for her veterans.

After television became popular, she noted that Bethesda Naval Hospital didn't have one in the veterans' wardroom. She went to Baltimore and visited many stores that carried TVs. No luck. She then went into a jewelry store and explained her purpose. The owner bought a top-of-the-line model and had it delivered.

Every president from Franklin Roosevelt to Ronald Reagan took special note of her work. President and Mrs. Reagan sent her a birthday greeting in 1984, a message that prompted her to exclaim, "How did they know it was my birthday?"

During the last three years of her life, she was unable to travel, and it "broke her heart" that no one took up the mantle she had worn for nearly fifty years. But the memories of the smiles she evoked from "her boys" comforted her.

Mother Clarke died on April 21, 1987, at Meridian Nursing Home in Frederick. She was buried at Our Lady of Mount Carmel Cemetery in Thurmont after services at St. John the Evangelist Roman Catholic Church in Frederick. She was survived by ten children, forty-eight grandchildren and thirty great-grandchildren.

Martin Franklin Grove

Prospector and California Newspaper Pioneer

Speculation runs rampant when articles are written about Martin Franklin Grove. Details of his life are difficult to pin down with few exceptions. The only certainties are that he was the son of George W. and Elizabeth Biser Grove and that he was born in Middletown on January 18, 1826. He died on March 19, 1866, and is buried in the Union Cemetery in Burkittsville. He likely went by his middle name, as indicated by his tombstone, which lists him as M. Franklin Grove. But publications in California archives refer to him as either M.F. Grove or Martin F. Grove.

From there, almost all of his remarkable career is interspersed with conjecture. It is known that he was infected by gold fever after the discovery at Sutter's Mill near Coloma, California, in early 1848. As the mass migration

Gold miners during California's rush of 1849.

of those seeking their fortune in the gold fields ensued, Franklin enticed his brother Manassas Jacob Grove, then a prosperous owner of several local merchandise stores, to lend him $5,000. There are indications that this was the total of M.J. Grove's savings at the time.

Off to California Franklin went. It wasn't long before he formed an association with George Kenyon Fitch, a New Yorker who had extensive training as a newspaper editor and printer. Their mining efforts at Auburn, California, yielded them barely a living. So when the printing equipment Fitch had purchased in New Orleans arrived in San Francisco, the two easterners decided to establish a newspaper in Sacramento, believing that the Bay City already had too many papers.

Records indicate that Fitch, Grove and Loring Pickering opened Sacramento's *Transcript* in early 1850. It quickly became an overnight success. With thousands of miners thirsting for news from outside the community they knew so well, the *Transcript* made money for the owners from the very beginning. Of course, Fitch kept the lion's share of the profits because it was his equipment that was used for publishing the paper. Also, he was listed as the "editor and publisher" on the paper's masthead.

Two years later, after a merger with another Sacramento newspaper, Fitch and Pickering bought out Grove's interest, providing the young Marylander with a handsome sum of between $15,000 and $20,000. Grove, however, continued to work in the newspaper business with Fitch, who eventually sold the Sacramento paper and moved his operation to San Francisco. Grove apparently accompanied Fitch. The newspaper there was again successful, and Fitch and his equity partners sold out in 1856. For a few years, he left the publishing and printing business altogether. It was likely at this time that Grove returned to Frederick County, repaying his brother, M.J. Grove, every penny he had borrowed in 1848 with interest.

Until his death in March 1866, nothing more is known of the exploits of Martin Franklin Grove. When he died, he was just forty years old. Perhaps, had he lived longer, written records of his later life may have survived. Apparently there was not a published obituary. If there was, it has not survived the past 146 years.

URIAH SHOCKLEY

Conquering Challenges, Overcoming Obstacles

Although he lost his ability to hear because of scarlet fever when just nine months old, Uriah B. Shockley never let it slow him down. When he was just a year old, polio added a little hitch to his step. To generations of students at the Maryland School for the Deaf and to countless employees of the *Frederick News-Post*, he showed what determination and a positive outlook can make of a man. He was an inspiration, a man who never thought of his inability to hear the spoken word as a handicap or a disability.

He was born on December 19, 1897, in Manry, Virginia, and despite his early health setbacks, he grew to stand out in a crowd—well over six feet with a sturdy build. His hands were particularly impressive, dwarfing all with whom he shook hands.

When it was time for school, his mother traveled across the state to enroll him in the Virginia School for the Deaf and Blind. But it wasn't long before she realized that it wasn't the place for Uriah. Following the death of his railroading father, she moved the family to Frederick to take advantage of the Maryland School for the Deaf. It was fortuitous for both Uriah and Frederick. He excelled there and also met his wife, Bernice Pritchett, who was born deaf. They married in 1921 and raised three children at 834 North Market Street in Frederick.

G. Thomas Mills, the executive editor of the *News-Post*, delighted in recounting his initial meeting with Uriah: "The first time I met him in January 1968, he shook my hand with his friendly, powerful hands and penned this note to me: 'I have three children and

Uriah Shockley. *Courtesy of the Shockley family.*

five grandchildren…ALL SPEAKING AND HEARING.'" He was so proud of his offspring, and it always showed.

Uriah was the first deaf person to be granted a Maryland driver's license and was among the first deaf linotype operators in the state. No matter where he worked, he liked the night shift. Every employee who shared it with him came to know a man dedicated to his trade, a man who prided himself on a job well done. One of the most difficult jobs at every newspaper is the preparation of the classified section, particularly when it was produced in hot type. This was Uriah's job for fifty years, sometimes preparing as many as sixteen pages a night.

There is one story the family relates that shows his practicality. After Robert E. Delaplaine, then publisher of the *News-Post*, died in August 1955, his will contained a remarkable clause. He bequeathed $250 to every employee so they could purchase a watch. Uriah needed a new roof on his house, so that's what he did with the gift. Besides, he told others, he already had a watch.

Selected Bibliography

Andrews, Matthew Page. *Tercentenary History of Maryland*. 4 vols. Chicago: S.J. Clarke Publishing Company, 1925.

Cannon, Gorsline, and Whitmore Cannon. *A Pictorial History of Frederick Maryland: The First 250 Years 1745–1995*. N.p.: Key Publishing Group, 1995.

Engelbrecht, Jacob. *The Diary of Jacob Englebrecht, Historical Society of Frederick County, Inc*. Frederick, MD: Historical Society of Frederick County, 1975

Gordon, Paul, and Rita Gordon. *A Textbook History of Frederick County MD*. N.p.: Board of Education of Frederick County, 1975.

Microfilm files of the *Washington Post, Baltimore Sun, Valley Register, Catoctin Enterprise* and *Frederick Post* and the *News*. Located in the Maryland Room of the C. Burr Artz Library, Frederick.

Scharf, J. Thomas. *History of Western Maryland, Being a History of Frederick, Montgomery, Carroll, Washington, Allegany and Garrett Counties from the Earliest Period to the Present Day, Including Biographical Sketches of Their Representative Men*. 2 vols. Philadelphia: L.H. Everts, 1882.

Williams, Thomas J.C., and Folger McKinsey. *History of Frederick County: From the Earliest Settlements...to the Present Time*. 2 vols. N.p.: L.R. Titsworth & Co., 1910.

Notes on Sources

The files of the *Frederick Post* (1910–2013) and the *News* (1883–2013) were most helpful in generating clues to further investigation of the subjects detailed herein.

Historical societies and libraries in various states contributed as well, being most helpful in providing artwork and biographical information.

The collections of the Maryland Room of the C. Burr Artz Library in particular and a similar collection at the Historical Society of Frederick County were used, and my own personal collection of some four hundred volumes—far too extensive to list here.

About the Author

A native Virginian, John W. Ashbury attended both public and private schools before earning a bachelor's degree at Emory and Henry College. A journalist by trade and inclination, he worked for the *Frederick News-Post*, the *Sun* of Baltimore, the *Roanoke World-News*, the *Bloomington (IN) Tribune*, the *Raleigh (NC) News & Observer*, Baltimore's *Evening Sun* and the *Glade Times & Mountain Mirror* (Walkersville, MD). In 1997, he published a volume entitled *...and all our yesterdays: A Chronicle of Frederick County, Maryland* (Diversions Publications, Inc.), which in turn led to his contributions to *Frederick Magazine*, some of which are reproduced in this volume. He is married and has three children and six grandchildren, one of whom he hopes will inherit his love for the history of Frederick County, research of which cannot but help to add to the fabled stories of this magical place.

Visit us at
www.historypress.net

....

This title is also available as an e-book